COOKING WITH

Bon Appétit

COOKING WITH
Bon Appétit

Vegetables

THE KNAPP PRESS
Publishers
Los Angeles

Published by The Knapp Press
5900 Wilshire Boulevard, Los Angeles, California 90036

Library of Congress Cataloging in Publication Data

Main entry under title:

Vegetables.

  (Cooking with Bon appétit)
  Includes index.
  1. Vegetables. I. Bon appétit. II. Series.
TX801.V423   1983   641.6'5   83-10088
ISBN 0-89535-119-6

On the cover: *Carrots with Pistachios and Cointreau*

Printed and bound in the United States of America

10 9 8 7 6 5 4 3 2 1

❦ Contents

🍎 *Foreword*

Vegetables are the new celebrities of the food world. Ever since we discovered just how delicious they are when cooked only briefly—how they retain their vibrant colors, crisp textures and unique flavors—vegetables have been the subject of much glowing discussion. Cooks everywhere talk about when, where and how to buy them; about classic methods and new ways of preparing the best of the season's bounty.

With almost 200 favorite recipes from the pages of *Bon Appétit,* this book is an indispensible guide to the world of vegetables. Divided into seven chapters by vegetable categories—such as Greens, Shoots and Stalks; The Cabbage Family; and Squash—this volume is especially convenient when you're looking for just the right recipe for whatever vegetable is in season. Within the chapters, you can select from appetizers, such as Eggplant Caviar (page 65), to salads like Celeriac Rémoulade (page 18), from a basic broccoli stir-fry (page 21) to a delightfully unexpected combination like Corn Pudding Soufflé in Cabbage (page 43). And there are main dishes too. A slice or two of the Cauliflower and Ham Tart (page 29) or Zucchini Pizza (page 53) would satisfy even the heartiest of appetites. And the diversity in the final chapter, Mixed Vegetables, is found in the number of vegetable combinations as well as in the types of dishes represented—from pickles to purees, casseroles to quiches.

Throughout these pages, you'll find more than just fabulous recipes. Special features in each chapter provide invaluable information about the basics of vegetable preparation, advice on how to select perfect produce and hints on how to take advantage of local farmers' markets. One feature discusses 14 varieties of beans; another describes the best vegetables to use for stuffing and what to fill them with.

All in all, this volume is a celebration of the vegetable—the one that is coming out of the pan sooner, being imaginatively combined with herbs and spices, and taking its place proudly in almost every part of a menu. We present these vegetable recipes for your enjoyment and inspiration; and as a tribute to farm fresh, full-of-flavor produce. So, if the sight of tomatoes, carrots and peppers toppling in a waterfall of brilliant colors from a cart triggers your imagination, here is where you'll find recipes to spur you on with hundreds of new ideas.

1 🍋 Greens, Shoots and Stalks

Who can resist the delicious simplicity of a bowl of mixed greens? A salad is one of the quickest and most nutritious accompaniments to a meal, and with a little embellishment it can become a satisfying main course. But beyond their traditional use in salads, greens—spinach, kale, and chard—lend themselves to myriad other preparations.

The Moors called spinach the Prince of Vegetables, and it remains a perennial favorite. Kale and chard also have their devotées: Southerners in particular savor their crisp texture and the subtle nuance they lend to stuffing, gratins, soups, and stews. In this chapter, spinach, kale and chard are featured in recipes as varied as a simple sauté of kale, mushrooms and Dijon mustard (page 3), a spectacular entrée such as Gâteau Florentine (mornay-enhanced spinach and creamy mushroom fillings layered with crepes, page 7), and an easy-to-make Almond Spinach Roulade (page 9) or a Niçois Tart of Chard and Cheese (page 2).

Asparagus and artichokes could be called the ugly ducklings of the group, but asparagus is actually a member of the lily family—and those who have seen an artichoke in flower will attest to its beauty. Of course, anyone who has eaten either one knows they are both delicious and unique.

Artichokes are native to the Mediterranean, so the robust flavors of that area are particularly complementary to them, as in the artichokes marinated in an olive oil–orange juice sauce (page 10). Asparagus takes center stage in a series of dishes from all over the world: dressed with rice vinegar, soy sauce and ginger Japanese style (page 14) or in a maltaise sauce (page 15) from France.

Celery and the faintly anise-flavored fennel help round out this section. There is also the surprise of celery root—another ugly duckling often ignored at the grocery store. It has the crunch and flavor of celery with a texture somewhat like a parsnip—quite unusual and very delicious. Enjoy it in a lightly seasoned puree or cut it into matchsticks and toss with a zesty rémoulade sauce.

 *Greens*

Greens and Walnuts

5 to 6 servings

2 large bunches greens,* washed, trimmed and coarsely chopped
3 tablespoons olive oil
1 cup diced green onion
½ to 1 cup coarsely chopped walnuts

Salt and freshly ground pepper
Lemon wedges

Place greens in steamer over medium heat and cook just until limp. Transfer to bowl. Heat 2 tablespoons oil in medium skillet over medium-high heat. Add onion and walnuts and sauté until softened. Add to greens with remaining oil and toss to combine. Season with salt and pepper to taste. Serve with lemon wedges.

*Swiss chard, spinach, beet or turnip greens, or a combination of any greens may be used.

Niçois Tart of Chard and Cheese

Serve warm or at room temperature.

10 to 12 servings

Pastry
3 to 3½ cups all purpose flour
⅓ cup sugar
1½ teaspoons salt
1 cup (2 sticks) unsalted butter (well chilled), cut into small pieces
2 eggs

Filling
2 pounds (about 2 bunches) Swiss chard, tough white stems discarded
½ cup water

2 tablespoons (¼ stick) butter
1 tablespoon olive oil
2 cups thinly sliced leek, white part only (about 3 medium)
½ cup chopped fresh Italian parsley

½ cup golden raisins
2 teaspoons dried marjoram, crumbled
Freshly grated nutmeg
Salt and freshly ground pepper
4 eggs
½ cup whipping cream
1 teaspoon salt

¾ pound Fontina cheese, coarsely cubed
3 tablespoons butter, cut into small pieces

For pastry: Combine 3 cups flour with sugar and salt in processor and blend using on/off turns. Add butter and process using on/off turns until mixture resembles coarse meal. Add eggs and mix just until dough almost forms ball, adding remaining ½ cup flour 1 tablespoon at a time if mixture seems too wet. Shape dough into ball. Place between 2 sheets of waxed paper. Flatten dough into disc. Refrigerate several hours or overnight. *(Pastry dough can also be prepared by hand.)*

For filling: Coarsely chop chard. Transfer to large saucepan. Add ½ cup water. Place over medium-high heat, cover and cook until just wilted, 3 to 4 minutes. Drain well; squeeze dry.

Heat butter with oil in heavy large skillet over medium-high heat. Add leek and sauté until pale golden, 5 to 6 minutes. Stir in chard and cook until dry, 4 to

5 minutes. Blend in parsley, raisins and marjoram with nutmeg, salt and pepper to taste. Set aside to cool. Meanwhile, whisk eggs, cream and salt in medium bowl until well blended.

Preheat oven to 425°F. Roll dough out on lightly floured surface to thickness of ¼ inch. Fit into 11-inch tart or flan pan and trim edges. Flute decoratively or cut small leaf shapes out of trimmings and attach to rim, moistening dough with water if necessary to facilitate sticking. Line bottom with buttered parchment or aluminum foil. Fill with dried beans or pie weights. Continue baking until pastry is set, about 5 minutes. Remove beans and paper. Continue baking until pastry is golden brown. Cool crust on rack.

Preheat oven to 375°F. Spread chard mixture in prepared crust. Sprinkle with cubed cheese. Pour in egg mixture. Dot with remaining butter. Bake until heated through and slightly puffed, about 40 minutes. Cool on wire rack. Slice tart into thin wedges to serve.

Wilted Old South Greens

4 servings

½ pound bacon, diced
1 large onion, diced
2 garlic cloves, minced
1 tablespoon sugar
2 large bunches greens (mustard or turnip greens, kale, etc.), center stalks sliced into 2-inch lengths, leaves coarsely chopped

Hot Peppered Old South Vinegar (see following recipe)

Sauté bacon in large deep pot over medium heat until limp. Add onion and sauté until limp and pale golden. Add garlic and sugar and continue cooking. Add sliced stalks from greens and cook until limp. Add chopped greens all at once (along with any water clinging to leaves), cover and steam 2 to 3 minutes. Uncover, increase heat to high and cook until pan juices are reduced, about 2 minutes. Serve warm accompanied by cruet of vinegar.

Hot Peppered Old South Vinegar

In the South, it's traditional to keep a cruet of this vinegar on the table to sprinkle over wilted or steamed greens.

Makes 1 quart

¼ pound fresh green or red hot chili peppers

1 quart cider vinegar

Scald peppers in boiling water 60 seconds. Handling carefully, rinse under cold running water until cool. Place in 1-quart glass bottle or divide between two 1-pint glass cruets. Fill with vinegar. Cap and seal. Let stand in cool, dark area for 10 days to infuse, then remove peppers and discard.

Mushroom Mustard Kale

Kale, like mustard greens, has a strong, tangy flavor.

4 to 5 servings

3 tablespoons oil
1 medium onion, thinly sliced
1 cup sliced fresh mushrooms
1 garlic clove, mashed
1 large bunch kale (about 16 leaves), heavy stalks discarded, finely chopped

2 to 3 teaspoons Dijon mustard
Salt and freshly ground pepper

Heat oil in medium skillet over medium-high heat. Add onion and sauté until softened. Stir in mushrooms and garlic and sauté 2 to 3 minutes more. Reduce heat to low, mix in kale and cook covered about 15 minutes, or until kale is tender, stirring frequently. (If necessary, add a few tablespoons water so vegetables do not burn.) A few minutes before kale is cooked through, add mustard and salt and pepper to taste. Serve immediately.

Stuffed Swiss Chard

4 to 5 servings

12 to 15 large Swiss chard leaves

  5 tablespoons oil
  1 small onion, finely chopped
  2 garlic cloves, minced
  ⅓ cup minced parsley
  1 cup finely shredded cabbage
  1 cup chopped mushrooms
  2 cups cooked brown rice
  1 egg, beaten

  1 teaspoon dried oregano
    Salt and freshly ground pepper

  1 small onion, thinly sliced
  ¼ cup minced parsley
  1 32-ounce can tomato juice
  2 teaspoons cinnamon
1½ cups feta cheese, crumbled
    (optional)

Place chard in steamer over medium heat and cook only until limp enough to be rolled; set aside.

Heat 3 tablespoons oil in large skillet over medium-high heat. Add chopped onion, garlic and parsley and sauté until onion is softened. Stir in cabbage and mushrooms and sauté 3 to 4 minutes more. Mix in rice, egg and oregano, salt and pepper to taste.

Place 3 to 4 tablespoons of rice mixture in center of each leaf and roll envelope style, tucking in ends. Set aside.

Add remaining oil to 2- to 3-quart saucepan. Place over medium-high heat, add onion and parsley and sauté until onion is softened. Stir in tomato juice and cinnamon. Carefully lay stuffed leaves, seam side down, in sauce. Cover and simmer 20 minutes. Transfer to serving bowl and sprinkle with feta.

Watercress Walnut Salad

2 servings

  1 bunch watercress, washed and
    drained, heavy stems removed
  ½ cup walnut halves
  1 tablespoon minced green onion
    (optional)

  1 teaspoon wine vinegar
  ¼ teaspoon Dijon mustard
    Salt and freshly ground pepper

Dressing
  4 teaspoons walnut oil

Combine watercress, walnut halves and onion in bowl. Whisk together walnut oil, vinegar, mustard and salt and pepper to taste. Just before serving toss watercress mixture with dressing.

 Spinach

Spinach Pesto with Pasta

4 servings

3 cups loosely packed fresh spinach leaves, stems discarded
2 cups fresh parsley (preferably Italian flat-leaf type)
½ cup grated Parmesan cheese
½ cup grated Romano cheese
½ cup oil
¼ cup blanched almonds
¼ cup (½ stick) butter, melted
2 tablespoons pine nuts

3 large garlic cloves, crushed
1 teaspoon salt

1 teaspoon oil
Salt
1 pound pasta

Grated Parmesan cheese

Puree first 10 ingredients in blender or processor until smooth; set aside.
    Bring water to boil in large pan. Add oil and salt. Add pasta and cook over medium-high heat until al dente. Strain through colander, reserving ⅓ cup liquid. Blend hot liquid into puree and toss with pasta. Serve with Parmesan cheese.

Spinach, Catalonian Style (Espinacas à la Catalana)

8 servings

2½ pounds fresh spinach (about 2½ large bunches), stemmed

3 tablespoons olive oil

⅔ cup pine nuts
⅓ cup (generous) raisins
Salt and freshly ground pepper

Wash spinach thoroughly. Shake to remove excess water. Fill Dutch oven with spinach. Place over low heat and cook until wilted, stirring frequently and gradually adding remaining spinach, about 5 minutes. Drain well; squeeze dry.
    Heat olive oil in large skillet over medium-high heat. Add pine nuts and raisins and sauté 3 to 4 minutes. Add spinach with salt and pepper to taste and toss gently. Transfer to dish and serve immediately.

Sautéed Spinach with Pear

4 servings

1 teaspoon butter
3 tablespoons minced shallot
1 pound fresh spinach, cooked until just wilted, squeezed dry and finely chopped
1 ripe pear, peeled, cored and finely chopped

Generous pinch of freshly grated nutmeg
Salt and freshly ground pepper

Melt butter in large saucepan over medium-high heat. Add shallot and cook until golden. Blend in spinach, pear, nutmeg and salt and pepper. Cook, stirring constantly, until heated through. Serve immediately.

Lebanese Spinach

4 servings

1½ cups chicken stock
1 cup bulgur
1 cup cooked spinach, chopped

¼ cup plain yogurt
Salt and freshly ground pepper

Combine stock and bulgur in medium saucepan over low heat and cook until bulgur is al dente, about 10 to 12 minutes; *do not overcook*. Mix in spinach and yogurt and continue cooking until heated through. Season with salt and pepper.

Spinach Loaf à la Bernoise

Spinach Loaf à la Bernoise goes well with roasts, grilled or sautéed chicken or veal.

8 to 10 servings

2 large bunches spinach, well washed, stems removed
2 tablespoons (¼ stick) unsalted butter
¼ cup finely minced green onion

2 eggs
2 egg yolks
1 cup half and half
½ cup breadcrumbs
2 to 3 tablespoons freshly grated Parmesan cheese
Pinch of nutmeg

Salt and freshly ground pepper
2 tablespoons (¼ stick) unsalted butter
½ pound mushroom caps, quartered
1 cup whipping cream
Salt and freshly ground pepper
1 tablespoon butter and 1 tablespoon flour mixed into smooth paste
2 tablespoons finely minced chives

Cook spinach in rapidly boiling salted water 2 to 3 minutes. Drain thoroughly. When cool enough to handle, squeeze out all remaining moisture. Finely mince spinach and transfer to large mixing bowl.

Preheat oven to 350°F. Generously butter 9 × 5-inch loaf pan and line with buttered waxed paper. Melt 2 tablespoons butter in small heavy skillet over medium heat. Add green onion and sauté 2 to 3 minutes, until softened but not browned. Add to spinach.

Combine eggs, egg yolks and half and half in small mixing bowl and blend thoroughly with whisk. Add to spinach mixture together with breadcrumbs, Parmesan, nutmeg, salt and pepper. Spoon into prepared loaf pan and place in larger baking dish. Add boiling water to outer dish to depth of 1 inch. Cover loaf pan loosely with foil and bake 50 minutes or until knife inserted in center comes out clean. Remove from oven and set aside.

Melt remaining 2 tablespoons butter in large skillet over medium heat. Add mushrooms and sauté 2 to 3 minutes until nicely browned. Add cream and salt and pepper and bring to boil. Gradually whisk in bits of butter-flour mixture, beating constantly until sauce lightly coats spoon. Remove from heat immediately and stir in chives.

Run knife around edges of spinach loaf and unmold onto rectangular serving platter. Discard waxed paper. Cut loaf into ½-inch slices. Spoon mushroom sauce over loaf and serve immediately as appetizer or accompaniment.

Gâteau Florentine

8 servings

Spinach Filling
- 2 tablespoons (¼ stick) butter
- 1 tablespoon minced green onion
- 1½ cups chopped blanched fresh spinach or 1½ cups thawed frozen chopped spinach, squeezed dry
- ¼ teaspoon salt
- 2½ cups mornay sauce (use your favorite recipe)

Mushroom Filling
- 1 tablespoon butter
- 1½ teaspoons vegetable oil
- ⅓ pound mushrooms, chopped
- 1 tablespoon minced green onion
- 1 8-ounce package cream cheese, room temperature
- 1 egg
- ½ cup shredded Swiss cheese
  Salt and freshly ground pepper

- 8 10-inch crepes

Chopped fresh parsley (garnish)

For spinach filling: Melt butter in medium saucepan over medium heat. Add onion and sauté briefly. Stir in spinach and salt and cook until heated through, about 2 to 3 minutes. Stir in ½ cup mornay. Set aside.

For mushroom filling: Heat butter and oil in small skillet over medium-high heat. Add mushrooms and onion and sauté until golden, about 5 to 6 minutes. Beat cream cheese, egg and Swiss cheese in medium bowl until well blended. Season with salt and pepper. Stir in mushrooms and onion.

Preheat oven to 350°F. Generously butter 12-inch round baking dish. Place crepe in bottom of dish and spread with ¼ of spinach filling. Top with second crepe and spread with ⅓ of mushroom filling. Repeat layering, ending with crepe. Cover with remaining mornay sauce. Bake until hot and bubbly, about 25 to 30 minutes. Sprinkle with parsley. Cut into wedges and serve immediately.

Spinach Cheese Casserole

4 to 6 servings

- 1 10-ounce package frozen chopped spinach, thawed and squeezed dry
- 8 ounces grated Gruyère or Swiss cheese
- 6 eggs, lightly beaten
- 2 slices day-old bread (crusts trimmed), torn into pieces
- 4 teaspoons grated onion
- ½ teaspoon salt
- ¼ teaspoon freshly ground pepper
- ¼ teaspoon nutmeg

Sour cream (garnish)

Preheat oven to 350°F. Butter 8-inch pie plate. Combine all ingredients except sour cream in large bowl. Turn into pie plate. Bake until tester inserted in center comes out clean, about 30 minutes. Let cool slightly. Slice into wedges. Garnish each serving with dollop of sour cream.

Spinach Cheese Casserole can also be served cold.

Spinach Chausson

4 servings

Pastry
- 8 ounces pastry flour or all purpose flour (about 2 cups)
- ¾ cup (1½ sticks) chilled unsalted butter, cut into ½-inch pieces
- 1 egg
- 3 tablespoons ice water
- 1 teaspoon chopped fresh tarragon or ½ teaspoon dried, crumbled
- 1 teaspoon chopped fresh oregano or ½ teaspoon dried, crumbled
- 1 teaspoon chopped fresh chives
- ¼ teaspoon salt

Filling
- 1 jumbo or 2 medium artichokes, preferably with stems
- 1 pound fresh spinach, stemmed
- 2 tablespoons (¼ stick) unsalted butter
- 1 medium-large leek (white part only), thinly sliced and cleaned (2 generous cups)
- ¼ pound mushrooms, thinly sliced
- 2 ounces cream cheese
- ¼ cup whipping cream
- 1 small garlic clove, minced
- 1½ teaspoons fresh lemon juice
- ½ teaspoon minced fresh chives
- ¼ teaspoon minced fresh tarragon
  Salt and freshly ground pepper
  Freshly grated nutmeg
- 3 tablespoons freshly grated Parmesan cheese

- 1 egg, lightly beaten

For pastry: Combine flour and butter in large bowl and blend until mixture resembles coarse meal. Make well in center. Add egg, ice water, herbs and salt to well and blend with fork, then quickly mix with flour to form dough. Shape dough into ball. Turn out onto lightly floured work surface and flatten into disc. Wrap dough in plastic and refrigerate at least 1 hour.

For filling: Steam artichoke until bottom is tender when pierced with knife, about 45 minutes. Remove leaves and reserve for another use. Discard choke. Chop heart coarsely. Peel stem down to smooth inner core and cut core into ¼-inch-thick slices. Set aside.

Rinse spinach and shake lightly to remove excess water. Heat heavy large saucepan over medium-high heat. Gradually add spinach and cook, stirring constantly, until wilted, about 2 minutes. Let cool. Squeeze spinach dry; chop coarsely. Melt 2 tablespoons butter in same saucepan over low heat. Add leek. Cover and cook until almost tender, about 15 minutes, stirring frequently. Add mushrooms, increase heat to medium high and cook, stirring, until mushrooms are tender and liquid has evaporated, about 5 minutes. Add reserved artichoke heart and stem, spinach, cream cheese, whipping cream and garlic and cook, stirring, until cheese is melted and cream is absorbed, about 3 minutes. Remove from heat. Blend in lemon juice, chives and tarragon. Season with salt, pepper and nutmeg. Cool completely, about 30 minutes. Stir in Parmesan.

Grease large baking sheet. Roll pastry out on lightly floured surface into 15-inch circle about ¹⁄₁₆ inch thick. Roll up on rolling pin and transfer to prepared baking sheet. Spoon filling onto half of circle, leaving ½-inch border. Brush border with beaten egg. Fold unfilled half of pastry over top, covering filling completely. Trim edge with fluted pastry wheel if desired, reserving trimmings for decorating top. Press edges together to seal and crimp with fork tines. Brush top with beaten egg. Decorate with dough trimmings. Chill for at least 30 minutes.

Preheat oven to 375°F. Brush turnover generously with beaten egg. Bake until golden brown, about 30 minutes. Transfer to rack and cool at least 5 minutes. Serve hot or warm.

Almond Spinach Roulade

6 servings

Pancake
2 tablespoons (¼ stick) butter, melted
1 cup sifted all purpose flour
1 teaspoon baking powder
½ teaspoon salt
2 cups milk
2 eggs

Herbed Spinach Filling
5 tablespoons butter
½ cup chopped almonds
¼ cup chopped onion
1 tablespoon all purpose flour
¼ teaspoon dried thyme, crumbled

¼ teaspoon salt
⅛ teaspoon freshly grated nutmeg
Pinch of freshly ground pepper
1 10-ounce package frozen chopped spinach, thawed and drained

2 cups shredded cheddar cheese

1 cup sour cream
½ to 1 tablespoon Dijon mustard

For pancake: Preheat oven to 375°F. Line 10 × 15-inch jelly roll pan with foil, allowing overlap on sides and ends. Brush 2 tablespoons butter evenly over foil, including overlap. Sift flour, baking powder and salt into large bowl of electric mixer. Add milk and eggs and beat until smooth. Pour batter into prepared pan, spreading evenly. Bake until barely brown, about 23 to 25 minutes.

Meanwhile, prepare filling: Melt 2 tablespoons butter in medium skillet over medium-high heat. Add almonds and onion and sauté until nuts are lightly toasted, about 10 minutes. Stir in flour, thyme, salt, nutmeg and pepper and cook 1 minute. Add spinach and continue cooking 5 minutes, stirring constantly. Remove from heat and set aside.

Remove pancake from oven. Cover pan with towel, then top with large cutting board, if desired. Invert pancake onto towel and board or other flat surface. Remove pan and gently peel off foil. Spread filling evenly over pancake. Sprinkle cheese over top. Carefully roll up pancake lengthwise. Let stand 10 minutes. *(Roulade can be prepared ahead to this point, cooled, wrapped and refrigerated or frozen.)*

Combine sour cream and mustard in small serving bowl. Set aside. Slice roulade evenly into 6 pieces. Melt remaining 3 tablespoons butter in large skillet over medium-high heat. Add sliced roulade and sauté until lightly browned. Serve immediately. Pass sour cream separately.

Spinach Noodle Bake

8 servings

2 pounds fresh spinach, cooked just until wilted, drained and chopped, or 2 10½-ounce packages frozen chopped spinach, thawed and squeezed dry
1 pound penne or ziti noodles, freshly cooked and drained
1 pound ricotta cheese

2 15½-ounce jars marinara sauce
3 eggs, lightly beaten
⅔ cup freshly grated Parmesan cheese
⅓ cup chopped fresh parsley
2 teaspoons salt
½ teaspoon freshly ground pepper

Preheat oven to 350°F. Generously butter 3-quart casserole or baking dish. Combine all ingredients in large mixing bowl and blend thoroughly. Turn into prepared dish and bake until top is golden brown and sauce is bubbly, 25 to 30 minutes.

Creamed Spinach

4 to 6 servings

2 slices bacon, diced
2 tablespoons (¼ stick) butter
1½ tablespoons flour
1 cup half and half, scalding hot
1 pound cooked fresh spinach, finely chopped (about 4 bunches)

1 onion, diced and lightly sautéed in butter or oil
¼ teaspoon salt
⅛ teaspoon freshly grated nutmeg

Sauté bacon in medium saucepan until crisp. Reduce heat to medium low and add butter. When melted, whisk in flour to make a roux. Cook 2 minutes, stirring constantly. Slowly add hot half and half, whisking constantly until sauce is smooth and thickened. Simmer about 10 minutes, stirring frequently. Blend in remaining ingredients and heat through.

 *Artichokes*

Marinated Artichokes

Orange juice and herbs combine for a distinctively different marinade.

2 servings

2 artichokes, cooked

Marinade
½ cup orange juice
¼ cup olive oil
2 tablespoons tarragon vinegar
2 tablespoons chopped shallot or green onion
1 tablespoon minced fresh parsley

1½ teaspoons grated orange peel
½ teaspoon salt
Pinch *each* of sugar, tarragon, basil and chervil
¼ teaspoon dry mustard
¼ teaspoon Worcestershire sauce

Cut artichokes in half from tip to stem. Remove choke and small inner leaves.
Combine all ingredients for marinade in medium bowl and blend well. Add artichokes, turning several times to coat. Cover and refrigerate overnight. Serve artichokes with some of marinade spooned over top.

Artichoke Vinaigrette
(Artichaut en Feuilles Vinaigrette)

6 first-course servings

6 large artichokes
2 small lemons, halved

½ cup white wine vinegar or shallot vinegar
1 tablespoon Dijon mustard
1 egg yolk
¾ cup olive oil
¾ cup safflower oil
Salt and freshly ground white pepper

24 2-inch-long Belgian endive tips
3 hard-cooked eggs, finely chopped

6 large radishes, sliced paper thin (garnish)
Very thinly sliced truffles (optional garnish)

Cut off stems at base of artichokes and discard. Using kitchen shears, snip thorny tips from all outside leaves. Immediately rub cut surfaces with lemon half to prevent discoloration. Bring about 3 quarts salted water to rapid boil in nonaluminum stockpot. Squeeze juice of lemon halves into pot; drop in shells. Add artichokes. Cover and cook until tender, about 40 minutes. Remove artichokes with slotted spoon. Set aside to cool.

Meanwhile, blend vinegar, mustard and yolk in small bowl. Whisk in oils 1 drop at a time. Season to taste with salt and freshly ground white pepper.

Remove 4 outside leaves from each artichoke; cut trimmed ends to points for garnish. Arrange remaining leaves in overlapping circle around rims of individual plates, dividing evenly. Cut off tight cone of tender inner leaves just above artichoke bottom. Remove and discard choke. Trim edges and quarter each artichoke bottom. Arrange in center of plates just inside circle of leaves. Set 4 endive tips over artichoke bottoms, spacing evenly. Set reserved artichoke leaves between endive tips. Mound chopped egg in center. Arrange radish slices upright in egg in circular fashion, bending each slice slightly to form flower petal design. Roll up 1 radish slice and place in center. Garnish endive tips with sliced truffles and serve. Rewhisk dressing thoroughly and pass separately.

Artful Artichokes

4 servings

⅔ cup mayonnaise
¼ cup (½ stick) butter, melted
2 tablespoons fresh lemon juice
½ teaspoon celery salt
1 15-ounce can artichoke hearts (packed in water), drained

¼ cup slivered almonds
¼ cup grated Parmesan cheese

Preheat oven to 425°F. Combine first 4 ingredients in small saucepan and whip until smooth. Place over low heat, stirring constantly until heated through; *do not boil*. Arrange artichokes in shallow baking dish just large enough to accommodate in single layer. Pour sauce over top. Sprinkle with almonds and cheese. Bake until heated through, about 10 minutes.

🌱 Artichokes

The adaptable artichoke—it fits in almost anywhere. It can be served as a first course, used alone as a featured vegetable or mixed with another. Moreover, artichokes are one happy exception to the rule that everything delicious is fattening. A medium trimmed specimen is listed at about 58 calories and 7 grams of carbohydrates and is rich in vitamins and minerals.

Virtually all American artichokes now come from the fields around Castroville, California, near Monterey, the landscape of many of John Steinbeck's novels. The frosts and cotton-batting fogs of this coast sometimes produce the tender "winter-kissed" artichokes, identifiable by their bronze-tinted leaves. The heaviest supplies of good artichokes (and the lowest prices) hit the markets in April and May. Good qualities to look for are firm heads and leaves that are open slightly. Artichokes should yield a bit when pressed.

Size has nothing to do with quality, but it can be a consideration in determining style of preparation. In general, large artichokes are the best for stuffing, medium work well in salads, small ones are good for pickling and frying. When a recipe calls for baby artichokes, don't substitute large. (Even with baby artichokes, it is necessary to peel off some of the outside leaves to get down to the delicious, tender pale green leaves surrounding the choke.)

Raw artichokes do not keep well. If you must store them for a day or two, put them in refrigerator vegetable drawers where humidity will slow wilting. Cooked, they keep for several days if refrigerated in a covered container.

The mystique surrounding the proper way to eat an artichoke has long kept the timid from sampling its delights. Perhaps the following will reveal that the etiquette involved springs from logic rather than a social arbiter's notion of daintiness.

Pull off a leaf and dip it in sauce (this will be anything from melted butter with lemon juice to hollandaise, mayonnaise, sour cream or vinaigrette). Pull the base of the leaf through your closed teeth. Discard the tough end of the leaf. Use a knife and fork when you come to the succulent bottom, or crown.

Step-by-Step Directions for Preparing Artichokes

Lay each artichoke on its side on cutting surface. Slice off stem at base to leave smooth bottom. Remove any tough or discolored bottom leaves. Cut off about an inch or so of top leaves. Using kitchen shears, trim any remaining tips from leaves. Rub base and all cut portions of artichoke with half a lemon to prevent discoloration. *Carbon steel knives should not be used; they will discolor artichokes and give them a metallic taste.*

Add enough water to a large mixing bowl to cover artichokes as they are prepared. Add juice of half a lemon to make acidulated water. Using fingers, open up center of each artichoke and push leaves apart. With melon scoop or sturdy teaspoon, remove and discard fuzzy choke, scraping to clean thoroughly. As artichokes are cleaned, drop them into acidulated water. The artichokes are now ready to be cooked.

The choke may also be removed after artichokes have been either parboiled or fully cooked. You might choose to attend to this ahead of time so they can be served hot, but some people may find them easier to "de-fuzz" after they're cooked.

🌱

How to Cook Artichokes

4 servings

1 gallon water
2 teaspoons salt
4 to 6 tablespoons lemon juice or vinegar
½ to 1 tablespoon olive oil or more to taste
1 to 2 bay leaves (optional)
10 to 12 whole peppercorns

4 large trimmed artichokes (4 inches in diameter before trimming) or 6 to 8 medium artichokes (2¾ inches to 3¾ inches in diameter before trimming)

Combine all ingredients except artichokes in a 5-quart pan and bring to boil. Add artichokes, partially cover with lid and return to boil. Cook until stem end is easily pierced with a fork, allowing about 25 to 30 minutes for medium and 40 to 50 minutes for large artichokes.

Remove from liquid and drain upside down. Serve hot or cold as desired.

Artichokes may also be cooked in advance. Reheat by returning them to the simmering liquid 5 to 10 minutes or until heated through.

They will keep several days covered in the refrigerator.

Use an enamel or stainless-steel pan for cooking artichokes. Do not use cast iron or aluminum utensils, since they will discolor artichokes and give them a metallic taste.

How to Cook Artichoke Bottoms (Crowns)

4 servings

1 tablespoon all purpose flour
2 cups water
1 lemon, halved

4 large artichokes (about 1¼ pounds each before trimming)

Prepare *blanc légume,* or vegetable whitener, by sifting flour through a sieve into large pan. Pour water over flour (this prevents lumping). Shake sieve in water to dissolve any remaining flour. Stir in juice of half the lemon.

Cut off artichoke stems at base to leave a smooth flat bottom. Trim away outer leaves of artichokes. Place each artichoke on its side and cut off remaining leaves. Neatly trim artichoke bottom's base, top and sides.

Rub remaining lemon over cut portions to prevent discoloration. As each artichoke bottom is prepared, drop into *blanc légume.* Bring to a boil, cover and simmer 30 minutes or until tender. Drain. Using a teaspoon or melon scoop, remove the fuzzy choke (center). The finished bottoms are ready for filling or marinating.

Butter Sauce for Artichokes

4 servings

1 cup (2 sticks) melted butter
¼ cup fresh lemon juice
¼ cup chopped fresh parsley

1 teaspoon salt
½ teaspoon dry mustard

Combine all ingredients and simmer 5 minutes. Serve warm as dipping sauce with hot artichokes.

 Asparagus

Prosciutto-Wrapped Asparagus

The fine delicate flavor of Italy's air-cured ham is a nice contrast with asparagus. If it is unavailable, substitute any thinly sliced cooked ham.

2 servings

16 asparagus spears
Melted butter (optional)

2 slices prosciutto

Snap off tough ends of asparagus and discard. Rinse spears well. Scrape with sharp knife to remove scaly leaf points. Arrange spears in single layer in large skillet and add enough boiling salted water to cover. Place over high heat and return water to boil, then reduce heat, cover and simmer until asparagus is tender, about 8 minutes. Drain. Drizzle lightly with melted butter if desired. Divide spears into 2 bundles and wrap each with slice of prosciutto.

Asparagus Salad with Cucumber Chrysanthemums (Asuparagusu Sunomono)

8 servings

Dressing
6 tablespoons rice vinegar
2 tablespoons mirin*
2 teaspoons light soy sauce
1 teaspoon finely minced fresh ginger

Salad
2 large cucumbers, peeled (ends trimmed)

Fresh spinach leaves
or leaf lettuce

2 pounds asparagus, cooked
8 large white mushrooms, sliced

8 small pieces red bell pepper or pimiento (optional garnish)

1 to 2 tablespoons toasted sesame seed

For dressing: Combine all ingredients in small bowl and blend well.

For salad: To form chrysanthemum, cut each cucumber crosswise into 4 equal pieces. Place 1 piece, cut side up, between 2 parallel chopsticks on work surface. Make parallel cuts ⅛ inch apart across entire cucumber piece, using chopsticks to keep knife from cutting completely through cucumber. Rotate cucumber 90 degrees and repeat cuts to form crosshatch design. Transfer to bowl of ice water. Repeat with remaining cucumber pieces.

Before serving, drain cucumber well on paper towels; pat dry. Press gently on cut surface to spread into flower shape. Place spinach or lettuce leaves on individual salad plates. Arrange cucumber, asparagus and mushroom slices decoratively on greens. Set piece of red pepper or pimiento in center of each cucumber flower if desired. Restir dressing and drizzle over salads. Sprinkle asparagus with toasted sesame seed.

* Available in oriental markets.

Asparagus Maltaise

Asparagus tips with orange hollandaise makes a color-ful first course.

4 to 6 appetizer servings

Maltaise Sauce
- 2 egg yolks
- 2 tablespoons plain yogurt
- 1 tablespoon fresh lemon juice
- 1 tablespoon dry Sherry
- ½ cup vegetable oil (preferably cold-pressed safflower)
- 1 tablespoon finely grated orange peel
- ⅛ teaspoon sea salt or ¼ teaspoon coarse salt

Ground red pepper

- 24 to 36 medium-size asparagus spears, well trimmed and cooked crisp-tender

For sauce: Combine egg yolks, yogurt, lemon juice and Sherry in small bowl and beat with small whisk. Set bowl in medium skillet half filled with hot water. Beat mixture over low heat until thick. Whisking constantly, gradually add oil in slow steady stream. Stir in orange peel, salt and pepper.

Transfer sauce to small bowl, set in center of serving platter and surround with asparagus spears.

Maltaise Sauce can be prepared up to 6 hours ahead. Let stand at room temperature or leave in warm water bath.

Celery and Fennel

Braised Fresh Celery

4 servings

- ½ cup chicken or veal stock
- ½ cup dry vermouth
- 2 tablespoons fresh lemon juice
- ¾ teaspoon fennel seed
- 8 black peppercorns
- 4 celery hearts, halved crosswise, then quartered lengthwise

- 4 teaspoons unsalted butter
- ¼ cup freshly grated Parmesan cheese
- ¼ cup fresh breadcrumbs

Combine stock, vermouth, lemon juice, fennel seed and peppercorns in large skillet over medium-high heat. Add celery hearts and simmer until just tender when pierced, about 15 to 20 minutes. Remove celery with slotted spoon. Continue simmering until liquid is reduced to ⅓ cup.

Preheat oven to 350°F. Coat small baking dish with 1 teaspoon butter. Transfer celery to baking dish. Pour reduced liquid over celery. Sprinkle with Parmesan and breadcrumbs. Dot with remaining 3 teaspoons butter. Bake until lightly golden, about 15 minutes. Serve immediately. Spoon any remaining liquid over celery.

🍎 Asparagus

We know that spring has come in earnest when the first asparagus appears in the market. Then we can delight in a cluster of pencil-slim, bright green spears cooked to tender crispness.

You might try sampling the white varieties of France and Germany—white because they are not exposed to the sun during their growing period. Europeans consider the white asparagus far superior to the green, while some others think of the white as lackluster. Unfortunately, the white is available here only in cans (with a few rare exceptions).

Americans often appear to be convinced that biggest is best. This may apply to a sirloin steak, but certainly the opposite is true of vegetables. In most cases the younger (therefore smaller) the vegetable, the better the flavor. Asparagus is a prime example.

When buying asparagus, look for thin spears with firm, closed compact tips. Limp tips indicate the vegetable isn't as fresh as it should be, and tips that are beginning to flower indicate harvesting was a little too late. Another way to check freshness is to examine the base of the stalks. They should have a moist, fresh-cut look to them. Make sure spears are uniform in size to ensure even cooking. You may have to ask your greengrocer to bundle them in uniform widths.

In addition to marvelously delicate flavor, thin asparagus offers another bonus—it does not require peeling. Just break or cut off and discard the tough section toward the bottom of each stalk.

If you are not going to use your asparagus immediately, store in a plastic bag, tip end first, and place in the vegetable section of the refrigerator. If very fresh, asparagus will hold well for up to two days. If they are in a borderline state between freshness and wilting, trim about an inch off the bottom of the stalks and place in a vaselike container. Pour in about an inch of water and cover lightly with plastic wrap. Refrigerate up to two days.

Harvesting Your Own—Wild or Tame

One way of guaranteeing a steady supply of fresh asparagus is to grow your own. This requires even more patience, two to three years' worth, to be exact. Start from seeds or one-year-old dormant roots. Plant in sundrenched, well-drained sandy soil. Allow stalks to go to seed for two or three years and then begin harvesting the following year. The reward for all this fortitude will be many years of gathering this luxurious vegetable.

Wild asparagus closely resembles its cultivated cousin and is easy to find. Its feathery, dill-like fronds can be found in sunny spots with sandy soil. Look for plants about three feet tall. If you part the stalks near the ground, you should find tender young asparagus poking their way through the earth. Once you've cut a basketful, give the plant a week's rest and then return. You'll find your patience has been rewarded by a new outcropping of shoots.

How to Cook Asparagus

Here are three proven methods of cooking asparagus. Just remember the cardinal rule—never overcook. When served cooked, asparagus should be bright green with a bit of crunch, never mushy or watery.

Method 1—Steaming

This method preserves almost all of the vegetable's nutrients. Fill the bottom of a 4-quart pot with 1 to 2 inches of water. Place a collapsible steamer basket in the pot. Bring water to a boil over high heat and place trimmed asparagus in a single layer. Cover pot and cook until asparagus shows only a little resistance when pierced with a knife. Time will vary from 3 to 8 minutes according to the size of the asparagus and how fresh they are. Lift steamer basket from pot and gently rinse asparagus with cold water to stop cooking and set color.

Method 2—Boiling

This works especially well with thin asparagus, since the tips are usually the same density as the stems. Half fill a large skillet with water. Bring to a boil over high heat and place asparagus in 1 to 2 layers (they should be covered with water). Boil until they show only a little resistance when pierced with a knife. Drain in a colander and rinse in cold water to stop cooking.

Method 3—The Coffeepot

Here's a technique that combines steaming and boiling and is ideal for thick asparagus. Use a tall percolator pot or asparagus cooker. Fill half full with water and bring to a boil. Tie asparagus in a bundle and lower into pot. Cover and cook until upper stems show a little resistance when pierced with a knife. Drain in a colander, then rinse with cold water to stop cooking and set color.

Celeriac Rémoulade

6 servings

1 cup mayonnaise
2 tablespoons lemon juice
1½ tablespoons prepared mustard (preferably Dijon or Dusseldorf)
3 large celery roots, peeled and cut into matchstick julienne

Salt and freshly ground pepper

1 tablespoon minced chives (garnish)

Combine first 3 ingredients in large bowl and mix well. Stir in celery root. Season to taste with salt and pepper. Chill well. Sprinkle with chives just before serving.

Fennel à la Grecque

6 to 8 servings

1 cup olive, peanut or corn oil
⅔ cup dry white wine or vermouth
⅔ cup white wine vinegar
2 teaspoons dried thyme, tarragon, oregano or basil, crumbled
2 teaspoons salt
2 large garlic cloves, halved crosswise

2 bay leaves
1 teaspoon freshly ground pepper
Dash of hot pepper sauce
6 medium fennel bulbs, trimmed and quartered

Combine oil, wine, vinegar, thyme, salt, garlic, bay leaves, pepper and hot pepper sauce in large skillet over medium heat. Add fennel and slowly bring to boil. Reduce heat and poach until fennel is crisp-tender when pierced with fork, turning frequently for even cooking. Taste broth and season with salt if desired. Cool fennel to room temperature in poaching liquid. Refrigerate until ready to use.

2 ❦ The Cabbage Family

Cabbage and its cousins—Brussels sprouts, cauliflower, and broccoli—have inspired cooks all over the world. France has its *choucroûte garnie,* Germany its hearty sauerkraut, and we have the all-American picnic favorite, coleslaw.

This chapter includes variations on all of these old-fashioned classics—including Caraway Red Cabbage Alsacienne (page 26), Sweet and Sour Cabbage (page 26) and Bleu Cheese Coleslaw (page 25)—plus some glamorous new updates. Try Feuilletés of Broccoli with Mushroom Sauce (page 21) or Mousseline of Broccoli (page 23) as the first course of an elegant dinner, or let the Balkan Spiral Pies with Cabbage Filling (page 28) star as the centerpiece of your next buffet or brunch. Stir-Fried Broccoli with Garlic and Lemon (page 21), or Dilled Brussels Sprouts (page 24) provide ways for dieters to enliven low-calorie meals.

Cabbage and these cabbage-type vegetables are among the oldest in recorded history. The subtle yet distinctive flavor of cabbage enables the cook to experiment with a variety of herbs and seasonings as the mood and menu dictate; caraway and pepper for a robust quality, or just a long simmering with a simple bouquet garni for a more delicate one. Besides being the basis for many eastern European soups and stews, cabbage leaves are also put to good use as wrappers for all sorts of fillings from meats, fish, or grains to a combination of other vegetables.

Brussels sprouts, cauliflower, and broccoli, on the other hand, have more pronounced flavors. That is why they are so often served lightly seasoned—perhaps sprinkled with breadcrumbs or drizzled with cream or béchamel sauce, allowing their natural tastes to come through.

As with all other vegetables, it is important not to overcook the cabbage family. Watch them carefully to be sure they retain their bright colors, crisp textures, and irresistible flavors.

 *Broccoli*

Broccoli in Oyster Sauce

6 to 8 servings

¾ cup chicken stock
1½ pounds broccoli, cut into florets, stems peeled and cut into 1-inch pieces

2 tablespoons peanut oil
1 tablespoon finely shredded fresh ginger

1 green onion, shredded
1 garlic clove, minced
1½ tablespoons oyster sauce*
½ teaspoon sugar
1 teaspoon cornstarch dissolved in 2 teaspoons stock (optional)

Bring stock to boil in medium saucepan. Add broccoli stems, cover and cook until crisp-tender, 3 to 4 minutes. Drain, reserving ½ cup stock.

Heat oil in wok or large skillet. Add ginger, onion and garlic and stir-fry 1 minute. Add broccoli stems and florets and stir-fry 2 minutes. Add oyster sauce, sugar and ½ cup stock and stir-fry 2 minutes. For thicker sauce, stir in dissolved cornstarch and cook briefly.

Asparagus can be substituted for broccoli.

*Available in oriental markets.

Broccoli with Pine Nuts

6 servings

2 pounds broccoli, peeled and cut into long stalks

2 tablespoons (¼ stick) butter

2 tablespoons pine nuts
1 tablespoon fresh lemon juice
Salt and freshly ground pepper

Fit large saucepan with steamer. Pour in enough water to come just below steamer and bring to rapid boil. Add broccoli, cover and steam until crisp-tender, about 8 to 10 minutes, depending on thickness of broccoli stalks. Rinse under cold water to stop cooking process. *(Broccoli can be cooked up to 1 day ahead and refrigerated).*

About 10 minutes before serving, melt butter in large skillet over medium heat. Add pine nuts and cook 3 minutes, stirring constantly. Add broccoli and cook until stalks begin to color slightly, turning occasionally and increasing heat if necessary. Transfer to serving platter. Sprinkle with lemon juice. Season with salt and pepper. Serve immediately.

For variation, steam broccoli leaves with stalks. Quickly sauté leaves in butter. Arrange leaves in single layer on serving platter. Top with steamed broccoli.

Broccoli Mushroom Stir-Fry

4 to 6 servings

1 large bunch broccoli
2 tablespoons olive oil
1 garlic clove, minced
¼ pound fresh mushrooms, sliced

¾ teaspoon salt
¼ cup freshly grated Parmesan
    cheese

Separate broccoli florets from stems. Peel stems and slice thinly. Place large skillet over high heat until very hot, about 30 seconds. Add oil and garlic and stir-fry 10 seconds. Add broccoli stems and stir-fry about 3 minutes. Add mushrooms and continue stirring about 1 minute. Add florets and salt and stir-fry 3 minutes. Transfer to heated platter and sprinkle with Parmesan. Serve immediately.

Stir-Fried Broccoli with Garlic and Lemon

4 servings

1 tablespoon olive oil
4 large garlic cloves, finely diced

3 cups broccoli (about 1 pound),
    sliced

½ cup water
Freshly ground pepper
Fresh lemon juice

Heat oil in wok or large skillet over medium heat. Add garlic and cook, stirring constantly, until golden, about 1 minute (do not burn). Remove garlic using slotted spoon and set aside.

Increase heat to high. When oil is very hot, add broccoli and stir-fry until it begins to brown. Add water and garlic. Cover and cook until broccoli is barely tender. Uncover and boil until liquid is evaporated. Season with pepper and lemon juice. Serve immediately.

Feuilletés of Broccoli with Mushroom Sauce

6 to 8 servings

1 large bunch fresh broccoli,
    trimmed and cut into florets

3 tablespoons unsalted butter
1 pound mushrooms, stemmed and
    sliced

1½ cups whipping cream
Beurre manié (1 tablespoon flour
and 1 tablespoon well-chilled
butter mashed to a paste)

2 tablespoons finely minced chives
Salt and freshly ground white
    pepper

6 to 8 feuilletés (see following
    recipe)

Bring salted water to boil in large saucepan. Add broccoli, reduce heat and simmer uncovered until just tender.

Melt butter in heavy-bottomed large skillet over medium-high heat. Add mushrooms and sauté until browned on both sides. Remove and set aside.

Add cream to skillet and bring to boil. Continue boiling until reduced by ¼. Add beurre manié a bit at a time and whisk constantly until sauce heavily coats spoon. Stir in chives. Return mushrooms to skillet and blend well. Season with salt and pepper to taste.

Divide broccoli among feuilletés and top with sauce. Serve immediately.

Classic Puff Pastry

Makes about 2 pounds of pastry or 1½ to 2 dozen feuilletés

3 cups all purpose flour
Pinch of salt
6 tablespoons (¾ stick) well-chilled unsalted butter, cut into small pieces
1 cup *ice cold* water

1½ cups (3 sticks) unsalted butter

1 egg beaten with 1 teaspoon water

Advance preparation: Place rolling pin (preferably ball-bearing type) in freezer until ready to prepare pastry.

Combine flour and salt in large bowl and blend well. Add 6 tablespoons butter and incorporate into flour with your hands until mixture resembles cornflakes. Add ice water and mix well. Knead dough until it is just smooth. (If dough is sticky, add a little more flour.) Wrap dough well in foil and chill in refrigerator for 15 minutes.

Meanwhile, knead remaining butter with your hands until it becomes a pliable ball. Set butter aside.

Lightly flour large work surface and the rolling pin. Roll chilled dough into a large square ¼ inch thick. Place kneaded butter in center and fold sides of dough over butter as if folding an envelope, enclosing butter completely. Flour the dough, transfer to plastic bag and refrigerate 30 minutes.

Lightly flour work surface and rolling pin again. Set dough in front of you so the line of the last fold is perpendicular to you and to the right of you. Roll dough into 18 × 8-inch rectangle approximately ¼ inch thick; do not roll completely to edges or butter may escape. When rectangle is 18 inches long, roll across entire surface of dough to flatten ends and achieve uniform thickness. Brush excess flour from dough. Fold dough in thirds as if you were folding a business letter, making sure that edges match up perfectly or there will be no uniformity in rising once the dough is baked. This completes the first "turn." Cover and refrigerate dough 1 hour or freeze 30 minutes. Dough should be firm but not hard.

Repeat procedure 4 times for a total of 5 turns, refrigerating dough 1 hour or freezing 30 minutes between each turn. Following the fifth turn, wrap and refrigerate the dough for 2 hours.

Position rack in center of oven and preheat to 425°F. Hold baking sheet briefly under cold running water. Shake off excess, then rub hand over sheet to make sure remaining water is evenly distributed. Line sheet with parchment.

With fold opening toward you, cut off 1-inch strip of dough using tip of sharp knife or pizza cutter. Roll strip into 12 × 2-inch rectangle ⅛ to ¼ inch thick. To promote even rising, trim ¼ inch of dough from each end.* Cut strip vertically into equal thirds. Turn rectangles upside down and place 2 inches apart on baking sheet. Repeat with remaining dough. Freeze 15 minutes. Brush rectangles with egg wash, being careful egg does not drip down sides of feuilletés or it will act as an adhesive and prevent pastry from rising evenly.

Bake until feuilletés are golden brown and have risen 3 to 3½ inches, about 20 to 25 minutes, watching carefully last several minutes to avoid burning on bottom. Cut each feuilleté in half horizontally and carefully remove and discard any uncooked pastry from center.

*Never discard puff pastry trimmings. They can be used for making any puff pastry that expands horizontally instead of vertically, such as *palmiers*. To maintain layering, piece them together edge to edge as you would a jigsaw puzzle rather than gathering into a ball. Roll out into new sheet of puff pastry ready for later use.

Broccoli Medallions with Peas

2 servings

1 tablespoon butter
1 cup thinly sliced peeled broccoli stems
½ cup tiny peas
¼ cup water
2 green onions (including some of green), sliced (about 3 tablespoons)

Salt and freshly ground pepper
2 teaspoons minced fresh parsley
½ teaspoon fresh lemon juice

Melt butter in large skillet over medium-high heat. Add broccoli, peas, water, green onion, salt and pepper. Cover and cook until vegetables are crisp-tender, about 5 minutes. Stir in parsley and lemon juice. Serve hot.

Mousseline of Broccoli with Mushroom Sauce (Mousseline de Broccoli au Sauce Morille)

Makes 9 or 10 half-cup molds

Mousseline
1 pound broccoli florets including ½ inch of stem

½ cup whipping cream
1 teaspoon salt
½ teaspoon freshly ground pepper
Pinch of nutmeg
Juice of ½ lemon
4 eggs

16 to 18 morels or other dried mushroom, well cleaned, rehydrated and halved or quartered
1 large shallot, minced

½ cup dry vermouth
1 cup whipping cream
Salt and freshly ground pepper
Lemon juice

Sauce
1 cup (2 sticks) unsalted butter

For mousseline: Generously butter ten ½-cup timbale molds or soufflé dishes. Bring large pot of salted water to boil. Add broccoli and cook until barely tender, about 10 to 12 minutes. Plunge into ice water to stop cooking process. Drain well. Preheat oven to 375°F.

Bring cream to boil in medium saucepan. Add broccoli, salt, pepper, nutmeg and lemon juice and mix well. Cook, stirring frequently, until cream is absorbed, about 10 minutes. Transfer to processor or blender and puree. Add eggs one at a time, mixing well after each addition. Taste and adjust seasoning.

Divide among prepared molds. Set in baking dish or shallow roasting pan and add hot water to come halfway up sides of molds. Cover molds with buttered foil. Bake until set, 25 to 30 minutes.

For sauce: Heat heavy medium saucepan over medium-low heat. Add 1 tablespoon butter, mushrooms and shallot and cook until all liquid is evaporated.

Meanwhile, cut remaining butter into small pieces and set aside.

Add vermouth to pan and cook over medium-high heat until liquid is reduced by half. Add cream and continue cooking until sauce is slightly thickened. Remove from heat. Using wooden spoon, stir in butter a few pieces at a time. Season with salt, pepper and lemon juice to taste.

To serve, run sharp knife around edge of molds and turn mousselines onto warm plates. Surround with sauce, nap tops lightly and serve immediately.

 *Brussels Sprouts*

Dilled Brussels Sprouts

Makes 2 to 2½ quarts

1½ pounds fresh brussels sprouts or
2 10-ounce packages frozen

2 cups cider vinegar
1 cup water
¾ cup sugar

¼ cup salt
2 garlic cloves, minced
1 large onion, thinly sliced
Fresh dill (1 sprig per jar)

Remove any brown or wilted outer leaves from brussels sprouts and trim stems. Wash well, place in steamer and steam until barely tender, about 8 to 10 minutes. *Do not overcook.*

Meanwhile, combine vinegar, water, sugar, salt and garlic in medium saucepan and bring to boil, stirring until sugar is dissolved. Layer sprouts and onion in sterilized jars. Tuck in dill. Pour hot vinegar mixture over and seal according to manufacturer's directions or refrigerate. Let stand a few days before serving.

Brussels Sprouts with Grilled Almonds (Choux de Bruxelles et Amandes Grillées)

6 servings

1½ pounds brussels sprouts
¼ cup (½ stick) butter
Salt and freshly ground pepper

⅓ cup roasted slivered almonds

Bring large amount of salted water to rapid boil. Meanwhile, remove and discard outer leaves of brussels sprouts. Cut shallow cross in root end of each sprout for even cooking. Boil until crisp-tender, about 8 minutes. Drain well. Melt butter in large skillet until dark golden brown. Remove from heat. Stir in sprouts with salt and pepper to taste. Sprinkle with nuts and serve.

Puree of Brussels Sprouts

10 servings

3 pounds brussels sprouts

6 tablespoons (¾ stick) butter, room temperature
1½ tablespoons whipping cream

Juice of 1 small lemon
1 teaspoon salt
½ teaspoon freshly ground pepper
Pinch of grated nutmeg

Bring large amount of salted water to rapid boil. Meanwhile, remove and discard outer leaves of brussels sprouts, trim stems and wash well. Boil 15 minutes, or until tender. Drain thoroughly and put through vegetable mill, or puree in blender or processor. *At this point, puree may be covered and refrigerated up to 1 day.*

Before serving, reheat puree over low heat. Stirring constantly, add butter, cream, lemon juice, salt, pepper and nutmeg. (The puree should be just soft enough to fall easily from a spoon.)

Puree may be kept warm up to 30 minutes in top of double boiler. Extra puree may be frozen and reheated.

From left: Quick Old-Fashioned
Corn Relish, Indian Pudding,
Green Corn Tamales

Irwin Horowitz

Asparagus Salad with Cucumber Chrysanthemums

French Peas, Carrot Ring, Steamed Cauliflower

Mousseline of Broccoli with Mushroom Sauce

Corn Pudding Soufflé in Cabbage with Sauce Nature

Pea Soufflé Roll with Minted Vegetable Sauce

Cauliflower and Ham Tart,
Braised Green Beans à la Basquaise

Chinese Salad, Rich Style

Dan Wolfe

 *Cabbage*

Bleu Cheese Coleslaw

4 to 6 servings

3 tart green apples, cored and chopped (about 5 cups)
3 to 5 cups thinly sliced cabbage
¼ pound bleu cheese, crumbled
1 cup sour cream
3 tablespoons grated cheddar cheese

1½ to 2 tablespoons thinly sliced green onion
1½ tablespoons fresh lemon juice
1 tablespoon chopped chives
1 tablespoon red wine vinegar
1 teaspoon salt
½ teaspoon freshly ground pepper

Combine all ingredients in large bowl and toss well. Cover and refrigerate until ready to serve.

Coleslaw-Filled Cabbage

8 servings

1 large cabbage
1 cup finely diced carrot
½ cup finely chopped onion
¼ cup chopped fresh parsley
2 tablespoons finely chopped green bell pepper

Dressing
½ cup oil
2 tablespoons all purpose flour

½ cup white wine vinegar
6 tablespoons sugar
2 teaspoons dry mustard
1 teaspoon salt
   Dash of hot pepper sauce
1 cup whipping cream
2 egg yolks

Core cabbage. Carefully remove 5 or 6 outer leaves without tearing and reserve *(if they are difficult to remove, hold cabbage under hot water several minutes until leaves are pliable)*. Halve remaining cabbage and slice very thinly. Combine in large bowl with carrot, onion, parsley and green pepper. Set aside.

For dressing: Combine oil and flour in small saucepan. Cook over medium heat several minutes, stirring constantly until mixture is smooth and slightly thickened. Stir in vinegar, sugar, mustard, salt and hot pepper sauce. Reduce heat to low. Whisk cream with yolks and gradually blend into vinegar mixture. Continue cooking, stirring constantly, until dressing is slightly thickened. Remove from heat and let cool 15 to 20 minutes (it will continue to thicken as it cools). Pour over cabbage mixture and toss thoroughly. Cover and refrigerate at least 1 hour or, preferably, overnight.

Line bowl with piece of cheesecloth or linen dish towel about same size as original head of cabbage. Set reserved outer leaves core end up in bowl, overlapping slightly. Drain cabbage mixture well, pressing or squeezing lightly to remove as much excess dressing as possible; reserve dressing to serve with slaw if desired. Carefully spoon coleslaw loosely into cabbage leaves, filling completely. Cover and refrigerate for 2 to 3 hours.

To serve, carefully lift cabbage from bowl using cloth liner as an aid and set onto serving dish; remove cloth.

For variation, add 1 cup cooked shrimp.

Recipe can be doubled for cabbage mixture; use same amount of dressing.

Caraway Red Cabbage Alsacienne

Serve with roast pork, duck or sausage.

6 servings

¼ cup (½ stick) unsalted butter
1 large onion, diced
2 Rome Beauty apples, peeled, cored and diced
1 3- to 4-pound red cabbage, shredded

2 tablespoons sugar
2 tablespoons brown sugar
½ teaspoon freshly grated nutmeg

¼ teaspoon ground cloves
½ cup dry white wine
¼ cup Caraway Seed Vinegar (see following recipe)
1 teaspoon salt
½ cup red currant or apple jelly

3 slices bacon, diced
2 tablespoons all purpose flour

Melt butter in large nonaluminum pot over medium heat. Add onion and sauté until tender and light golden. Add apple and sauté until soft and pale golden, about 5 minutes. Add cabbage and toss until well combined. Increase heat to medium high and cook until cabbage is limp, about 2 to 3 minutes.

Add sugars and sauté until they melt and begin to caramelize. Stir in spices, wine and vinegar and bring to boil. Cover partially, reduce heat to medium and continue cooking, stirring occasionally to prevent burning, until cabbage is tender, about 45 minutes. Season with salt. Blend in jelly, stirring until dissolved. Continue simmering gently, uncovered, 5 to 10 minutes.

Sauté bacon in small skillet until limp and slightly browned. Blend in flour and cook 1 to 2 minutes. Add to cabbage and cook, stirring, until thickened.

Caraway Seed Vinegar

Use in cabbage slaw, Caraway Red Cabbage Alsacienne or sauerbraten.

Makes about 1 quart

2 tablespoons caraway seed
1 quart red wine vinegar or cider vinegar

Gently bruise caraway seed using mortar and pestle. Place in center of 3-inch square of double-thickness cheesecloth and tie with string. Place in tall 1-quart glass bottle. Bring vinegar to simmer, then pour into bottle to fill. Cap and seal. Let stand in cool, dark area for about 10 days to infuse before using. Remove caraway seed and discard.

Sweet and Sour Cabbage

4 to 6 servings

2 tablespoons vinegar
2 tablespoons water
1 tablespoon sugar or more to taste
1 to 2 teaspoons soy sauce
½ teaspoon salt

¼ cup oil
1 small cabbage, cut into ¼-inch strips

Combine vinegar, water, sugar, soy sauce and salt in small bowl. Set aside. Heat oil in heavy medium skillet over medium-high heat. Add cabbage and stir-fry until crisp-tender, about 6 minutes. Stir in vinegar mixture and cook, stirring constantly, until cabbage is tender, about 3 to 5 minutes. Serve immediately.

❦ *Cabbage*

- Choose well-trimmed, solid heads, heavy for their size. Leaves should be firmly attached at the stem.
- Whole cabbages can be kept refrigerated in plastic bags for several weeks; shredded, about one week. Don't wash until ready to use.
- One medium head of cabbage (about 2½ pounds) yields sixteen 1-inch slices and about 9 cups shredded raw cabbage (7 cups cooked).
- The top half of the cabbage head is considered more tender and easier to shred. If it is practical, cut in half horizontally, using tops for salads, bottoms in cooked recipes.
- A whole, unshelled walnut dropped into the cabbage pot cuts down on cooking odors.
- Cabbage flavor is very compatible with anise, basil, caraway, celery seed, dill, mustard, fennel, nutmeg, oregano, savory and tarragon.
- Save cooking water for soups. It contains valuable nutrients.

Cabbage Noodles

10 to 12 servings

4½ pounds cabbage, cored and shredded
Salt
6 tablespoons (¾ stick) butter (or more)
6 tablespoons oil (or more)

¾ pound egg noodles, cooked al dente and drained
Freshly ground pepper

Arrange cabbage in colander and sprinkle with salt. Let stand 10 minutes. Squeeze dry. Melt 6 tablespoons butter with 6 tablespoons oil in large skillet over low heat. Add half of cabbage to skillet and sauté until crisp-tender. Stir in remaining cabbage and continue cooking until tender, about 15 minutes, adding more butter and oil if necessary (do not brown). Blend in noodles and heat through. Season with salt and pepper. Serve hot.

Carole's Cabbage Perrogen

Makes about 8 dozen

4 cups all purpose flour
2 tablespoons vegetable oil
1 teaspoon salt
1½ cups (about) water

1 medium cabbage (about 2 pounds), quartered and cored

¼ cup (½ stick) butter
1 yellow onion, chopped
Salt and freshly ground pepper

2 to 4 tablespoons (¼ to ½ stick) butter, melted

Combine flour and oil in large bowl. Dissolve salt in water. Add to flour mixture ½ cup at a time, blending with hands until dough is soft and pliable but not sticky. Form dough into ball. Wrap in waxed paper and refrigerate for 1 hour.

Fill Dutch oven with water and bring to boil. Add cabbage and continue boiling 5 minutes. Drain cabbage and chop coarsely. Melt ¼ cup butter in Dutch oven over medium-low heat. Add onion, cover and cook 10 minutes. Stir in chopped cabbage and cook, uncovered, for 10 minutes. Season with salt and pepper to taste.

Roll dough out on well-floured surface to thickness of about 1/32 inch. Cut dough into 3-inch circles using cutter or glass. Top each circle with small spoonful of cabbage mixture. Fold circles in half, carefully pressing sides together to seal.

Bring large pot of water to boil over high heat. Add perrogen (in batches if necessary; do not crowd) and boil until puffed and tender, 5 to 7 minutes. Drain well. Transfer to large serving bowl. Pour melted butter over top and serve.

Balkan Spiral Pies with Cabbage Filling

The savory cabbage filling is rolled in delicate phyllo pastry and shaped into individual spirals. Can be prepared up to 2 days ahead, baked just before serving and presented piping hot.

Makes 12 pastries

1 small cabbage (1½ to 2 pounds), quartered

2 tablespoons (¼ stick) unsalted butter

½ pound slab bacon, cut into ¼-inch dice

2 medium onions, finely diced

1 tablespoon sugar

2 tablespoons Hungarian sweet paprika

1 teaspoon caraway seed, crushed in mortar
Salt and freshly ground pepper

12 phyllo pastry sheets

1 cup (2 sticks) unsalted butter, melted

Bring large amount of water to rapid boil. Add cabbage and blanch 5 minutes. Drain well. Dry thoroughly, then press leaves to extract any remaining moisture. Cut cabbage into ½-inch-wide strips; discard heavy cores.

Melt 2 tablespoons butter in heavy large skillet over medium heat. Add bacon and cook until golden brown but not crisp. Remove bacon with slotted spoon; set aside. Add onion to skillet, increase heat to medium high and sauté until slightly wilted. Sprinkle with sugar and sauté briefly. Stir in shredded cabbage and sauté until softened, glossy and just beginning to color, 12 to 15 minutes. Season mixture with paprika, caraway, salt and freshly ground pepper. Return bacon to skillet and cook about 5 minutes to blend flavors. Set aside to cool.

Brush 1 phyllo sheet with melted butter. Fold sheet in half crosswise. Arrange ½-inch band of filling along folded edge, leaving 1-inch border on each side. Lightly brush pastry with butter. Roll pastry up, enclosing filling and forming long rope. Coil rope into spiral, tucking ends under and sealing with small amount of butter. Transfer to parchment-lined baking sheet. Repeat with remaining pastry. *(Pastries can be prepared to this point, covered and refrigerated.)*

Preheat oven to 375°F. Brush tops of spirals with melted butter. Bake until rich golden brown in color, 20 to 25 minutes. Serve immediately.

 Cauliflower

Cauliflower and Ham Tart

6 to 8 servings

Pastry
2 cups sifted all purpose flour
Generous pinch of salt
¾ cup (1½ sticks) unsalted butter, well chilled
4 to 5 tablespoons ice water

Flour

Filling
2 cups whipping cream
2 eggs
2 egg yolks

½ cup freshly grated Parmesan cheese
Salt and freshly ground white pepper

1 large cauliflower cut into florets (about 2 heaping cups)

2 tablespoons (¼ stick) unsalted butter
½ to 1 cup finely cubed smoked ham

By hand: Combine flour and salt in large mixing bowl and blend well. Gradually add butter and work with fingers until coarsely crumbled. Add 4 tablespoons water and knead dough until smooth, adding more water if necessary.

With processor: Insert Steel Knife. Combine ingredients for pastry; process until mixture just begins to form ball.

Flour dough lightly, wrap in waxed paper and chill 1 hour. When ready to roll out, preheat oven to 350°F. Place dough on lightly floured surface and roll into large circle ⅛ inch thick. Transfer dough to 10-inch quiche pan, pressing gently to fit bottom and sides. Trim off excess. Prick dough in several places with fork. Line with waxed paper and fill with dried beans. Place on baking sheet and bake 15 minutes. Remove from oven, lift out paper and beans. Return to oven for an additional 10 minutes to brown lightly. Let stand while preparing filling. Retain oven at 350°F.

For filling: Combine cream, eggs, yolks, Parmesan, salt and pepper in large mixing bowl and blend thoroughly. Set aside.

Bring salted water to boil in medium saucepan. Reduce heat to medium, add cauliflower and cook uncovered 3 to 5 minutes until barely tender. Drain thoroughly and run under cold water to stop cooking process.

Melt butter in large heavy skillet over medium heat. Add ham and sauté until lightly browned. Remove from skillet and reserve. Drain all but 2 tablespoons fat from skillet. Increase heat to high, add cauliflower and quickly sauté until lightly but evenly browned.

Distribute cauliflower and ham evenly over crust. Carefully pour custard over. Bake 40 to 45 minutes, or until knife inserted near center comes out clean.

Steamed Cauliflower

6 to 8 servings

1 large cauliflower
1 teaspoon salt

Paprika

Trim heavy outside leaves from cauliflower. Cut cauliflower into florets. Place in steamer or colander over boiling water. Steam covered 15 minutes or until crisp-tender. Sprinkle with salt. Just before serving, dust with paprika.

Calabrese Cauliflower

Makes about 5 quarts

3 large cauliflower, cut into bite-size florets
1 quart tiny pickling onions, peeled
1 cup chopped fresh parsley
½ cup chopped fresh mint
4 to 8 large garlic cloves, chopped

10 tiny dried red chilies
2 quarts water
1 quart white wine vinegar
¼ cup coarse salt

Bring large amount of salted water to rapid boil over high heat. Add cauliflower and parboil 3 minutes. Drain well. Transfer to large bowl. Add onions, parsley, mint and garlic.

Pack cauliflower mixture tightly into 10 clean, hot pint jars to ½ inch from top. Add 1 chili to each jar. Combine remaining ingredients in stockpot and bring to rapid boil. Ladle enough hot brine into 1 jar just to cover cauliflower mixture. Run plastic knife or spatula between vegetables and jar to release any air bubbles. Clean rim and threads of jar with damp cloth. Seal with new, scalded, very hot lid. Repeat with remaining jars.

Transfer to gently simmering (180°F to 190°F) water bath and process for 10 minutes. Let jars cool on rack. Test for seal. Store in cool dry place.

3 ❦ Legumes and Grains

Steaming bowls of baked beans, zesty Indian lentils, or a green bean casserole: legumes are the foundation of many satisfying, tempting recipes. As an inexpensive source of protein they have no equal, and the variety of textures and flavors they offer adds a wealth of delicious possibilities to the cook's repertoire.

There is plenty of robust, down-home fare offered in this chapter, but you will not find the selection limited to only that. For instance, Pea Soufflé Roll with Minted Vegetable Sauce (page 46) is a light and delicate accompaniment to grilled lamb or chicken, but it could also stand on its own as the focal point of a casual luncheon or late-night supper. Green Beans Provençal (page 40) and Green Bean Fritters (page 39) are delightful additions to any brunch or dinner.

But it is in ethnic favorites that legumes really excel. We suggest several here, including New Orleans' own Red Beans and Rice (page 37), Boston Baked Beans (page 33), Pasta and Beans, Tuscan Style (page 32) and Black Bean Dal (page 36). And note that although corn is a grain and not a legume, we have included it in this chapter because its rich taste is similar to the other dishes. Try Roasted Corn with Garlic-Parmesan Spread (page 42) at your next backyard barbecue. Country Corn Pudding (page 42) is excellent with ham and Green Corn Tamales (page 44) could easily serve as the main course of an informal dinner party for friends: Add a green salad and chilled bottles of beer and you're all set.

Legumes and corn are among the most plentiful vegetables. We hope these recipes add some intrigue to your menus and also help inspire new creations of your own.

 Dried Beans

Pasta and Beans, Tuscan Style
(Pasta e Fagioli Toscana)

This is Italian soul food at its best and one of the Milanese restaurant La Cantinetta's trademarks. Rustic, hearty and addictive, Pasta e Fagioli can be prepared in easy stages, making it ideal cold-weather party fare. Extra sauce can be refrigerated, then used later to dress pasta or rice or to spoon over seafood or meats.

8 servings

2 cups (14 ounces) dry cannellini beans (white kidney beans)* or Great Northern beans

1 garlic clove
1 large onion stuck with 2 cloves

¼ cup olive oil
2 medium onions, minced
2 large fresh rosemary sprigs or ½ teaspoon dried, crumbled
2 large fresh sage leaves or 2 dried
2 large garlic cloves, minced
1⅓ cups La Cantinetta Tomato Sauce (see following recipe)

3 quarts (about) meat or poultry stock

1 pound pappardelle noodles,* broken into medium pieces
Freshly ground pepper
2 cups freshly grated Parmigiano-Reggiano cheese

Combine beans in large saucepan with enough cold water to cover by about 3 inches. Set aside overnight.

Add garlic, whole onion and enough additional water to beans to cover by 3 inches. Bring to boil over high heat. Reduce heat and simmer until tender, about 2 hours. Discard onion and garlic. Set beans aside. *(Beans can be prepared up to 3 days ahead. Drain well, reserving about ½ cup liquid. Refrigerate beans and liquid until ready to use.)*

Heat oil in heavy nonaluminum 6-quart saucepan or stockpot over medium-high heat. Add minced onion with fresh rosemary and fresh sage (if using) and sauté until onion is golden, about 15 minutes. Discard fresh herbs. Add garlic with dried rosemary and dried sage (if using) and sauté 30 more seconds. Remove pan from heat. Puree enough beans with ⅓ cup reserved cooking liquid to measure 2 cups. Add pureed beans to onion mixture. Blend in tomato sauce. Place over low heat, cover partially and cook for about 30 minutes. Cool slightly.

Transfer mixture to processor or blender in batches and mix until smooth. Press mixture through sieve set over bowl. Return mixture to saucepan. Add about 2½ quarts stock and blend well. Place over medium heat and bring to gentle simmer. Cover partially and cook 30 to 45 minutes. *(Can be prepared up to 1 day ahead to this point, covered and refrigerated.)*

About 1 hour before serving, rewarm pureed bean mixture over medium heat, adding more stock as necessary to thin while cooking. Add pappardelle, cover partially and cook until pasta is firm but tender to the bite (al dente), about 15 minutes, stirring frequently and adding stock as necessary. Stir in remaining beans and continue cooking 15 minutes. *(Can be set aside for up to 30 minutes. Add more stock as necessary; finished dish should be consistency of thick soup.)* Taste and season generously with pepper. Serve in heated bowls. Pass cheese separately.

*Available at Italian markets.

La Cantinetta Tomato Sauce

Makes about 1 quart

¼ cup olive oil
1 medium onion, minced (about 1 cup)
1 small celery stalk, finely minced (about ⅓ cup)
1 small carrot, finely minced (about ¼ cup)
1 garlic clove, crushed
3 tablespoons minced Italian parsley

1 tablespoon minced fresh basil or 1 teaspoon dried, crumbled
¼ cup dry white wine
1 28-ounce can Italian plum tomatoes (undrained)
Salt and freshly ground pepper

Heat oil in heavy nonaluminum 3- to 4-quart saucepan over medium heat. Add onion, celery and carrot and cook until golden, stirring occasionally. Add garlic, parsley and fresh basil (if using) and cook until aromatic, about 1 to 2 minutes, stirring occasionally. Stir in dried basil (if using). Add wine and boil until evaporated. Blend in tomatoes and simmer 20 to 30 minutes, stirring occasionally to prevent sticking; sauce will be thick. Process sauce through food mill if smoother texture is desired. Season to taste with salt and pepper. *(Sauce can be prepared up to 5 days ahead and refrigerated.)*

Boston Baked Beans

This is a classic American dish with a heritage that goes back to the sturdy settlers of New England. This is but one way of making New England's famous dish. Although the optional rum might be considered heresy by some, here is one very nice pot of beans.

6 servings

1 pound (2½ cups) dried pea beans
Water

¼ pound lean salt pork, blanched
2 cloves
1 onion, peeled and halved

½ cup dark molasses

½ cup rum plus ½ cup reserved bean liquid, or 1 cup reserved bean liquid
1 tablespoon brown sugar
1 teaspoon salt
½ teaspoon dry mustard

Presoak beans 1 hour using quick-soaking method. (Boil 2 to 3 minutes. Remove from heat, cover and let soak for 1 hour.) Drain and transfer to large pot. Add enough water to cover by at least 2 inches and bring to boil. Reduce heat and simmer gently until tender, about 1½ hours. (Some bean "experts" say the beans are done when the skins burst if you blow on them.) Drain, reserving liquid.

Preheat oven to 300°F. Score salt pork every ½ inch with cuts 1 inch deep (or cut into chunks). Stick clove into each onion half and place in traditional bean pot or heavy 2-quart casserole with tight-fitting lid. Add beans. "Bury" salt pork in beans, leaving any rind exposed.

Combine molasses, rum and/or bean liquid, brown sugar, salt and mustard in small bowl and blend well. Pour over beans, adding enough additional reserved bean liquid to cover completely. Cover and bake 6 to 7 hours, adding more reserved bean liquid or water if needed to prevent beans from drying out. Remove cover, stir well and bake an additional hour.

🍎 Beans

The cinderella of the kitchen has always been the bean. While other foods are pampered and primped to be sent to the ball, the bean is left behind. One reason might be that beans are inexpensive, and some people consider their modest price a measure of their worth. Then, too, beans happen to be good for you, sometimes considered a questionable attribute. Beans are known to modestly reside on the dusty back shelf of the pantry, eventually becoming one of the kitchen fixtures, never noticed, never cooked.

Yet these sturdy legumes have a distinguished history. In Greek and Roman times, they were used to designate the votes in elections. A white bean meant yes, and a black bean signified that the rascals were on their way out. And, from time to time, beans have been used as currency, since they are easily transported and can be counted and divided.

Beyond their place in history, beans have long fulfilled a vital role in world cuisine. Since they are rich in protein, B vitamins, iron and calcium, they are important in cultures where not much meat is available. In China, as far back as the first century A.D., merchants made fortunes peddling bean relishes, and delicacies such as French *cassoulet,* Italian bean soups, Greek bean stews and Brazilian *feijoada* are all built around the bean.

An inspiring variety of dried beans is available:

Black, or turtle: These small oval beans with black skins and white interiors are popular in South America, the Caribbean and Mexico and are used in soups in the southern United States, where they are grown. Ham, green bell peppers and onions are all good flavorings for black beans.

Blackeye or yelloweye: These are called "peas" in the South. Tiny ovals with either a black or yellow spot, these beans are the basis for the South's famous Hopping John, a dish that combines them with rice and the flavors of ham, salt pork or bacon.

Chick-peas, or garbanzos: Also known as *ceci,* or Spanish beans, they have an irregular, almost rumpled-looking exterior, a firm texture and a nut-like flavor. Used in Spanish stews, Italian minestrone and Arab dip *hummus.*

Cranberry beans: These pink beans turn creamy white when cooked. They have a distinctive sweet flavor and are popular in Italian dishes.

Favas: These are Europe's most important beans. They have a slightly sharp flavor and are often cooked with bacon or ham.

Lentils: These mild-flavored, small grayish brown beans blend well with many foods. They require no presoaking, and they cook quickly.

Limas: Flat and kidney shaped, these beans appear in large and small varieties. Their buttery, nutlike flavor, which blends well with chicken, smoked meats or cheese, makes them one of the aristocrats of the bean family.

Pinto or pink beans: Although they don't look alike, these beans can be used interchangeably in recipes. The pinto is pale pink, speckled with brown; the pink bean is brownish red. Popular in the Southwest, both types accept forthright seasonings, such as chili powder, tomatoes and onions.

Red kidneys: Popular for chili and many Spanish dishes, these reddish purple beans are, next to soybeans, the most important in the world.

Soybeans: Both the smallest and the most often used bean, they can be yellow, green, brown, black or bicolored. They provide an invaluable source of nutrients in highly populated countries.

White beans are generally interchangeable:

Great northern: Delicate but distinctive in flavor, these are popular for all baked bean dishes.

Marrow: Largest and roundest of the white beans, marrow beans are used in soups and stews, and their flavor marries well with molasses, brown sugar and salt port.

Navy: Smaller than Great Northerns, navy beans are the ones commonly found in canned pork and beans.

Pea: The smallest of the white beans. New Englanders use these for their classic Boston baked beans.

Dried beans must be soaked to replace the water lost in drying. There are two ways to do this: Soak them overnight or resort to the quick-soaking method. For overnight soaking, rinse beans and pick over to remove any grit. For each pound, add 6 cups water. Soak overnight, drain and rinse.

For quick soaking, rinse beans and pick over to remove any grit. For each pound of dried beans, bring 2 quarts of water to the boil. Add beans and boil 2 minutes. Remove from heat, cover pan and soak at least 1 hour. Drain and rinse.

The cooking time for dried beans can't be pinpointed. It can vary depending on where they were grown, on their age, and on the hardness of the water in which they are cooked. Generally speaking, most beans will take 1½ to 2½ hours to cook, with lentils requiring less time and garbanzos more.

Salt the bean-cooking water (about 1 teaspoon per cup of dried beans) unless the dish includes ham, bacon, salt port or other salty meats. Adding a tablespoon of oil or butter for each cup of beans will reduce the foam as the beans cook. Most important, cook the beans over very low heat. Any violent motion will cause them to break. When you stir, use a gentle hand and a wooden spoon for the same reason.

To be sure you have beans ready when you are, you might want to precook some and store them in the refrigerator, where they'll keep for up to a week, or freeze them for incorporation into a dish at a later date. If you have cooked beans on hand, they can become a wonderful spur-of-the-moment salad with a dressing of oil and vinegar, herbs and a few chopped green onions. Or make an impromptu dip by putting cooked white beans or limas in a blender or processor with some olive oil, lemon juice and peeled clove of garlic. Whirl until smooth, season to taste and chill.

Black Bean Dal

6 to 8 servings

1 pound black beans
6 cups water
1 cup (2 sticks) butter
1 small garlic clove, chopped
2 teaspoons cumin seed
1 teaspoon ground coriander
1 teaspoon turmeric

1 teaspoon paprika
½ teaspoon ground ginger
  Salt and ground red pepper
1 cup whipping cream
  Rice or Indian bread

Rinse beans in colander under cold running water. Drain well. Transfer to 6- to 8-quart pot. Add water and bring to boil over high heat, skimming foam as it accumulates on surface. Add butter, garlic, spices, salt and red pepper. Reduce heat to low, cover and simmer until beans are tender, about 1 hour, adding cream near end of cooking time (mixture should be consistency of thick soup). *(Can be prepared ahead and refrigerated 5 to 6 days. Reheat before serving.)* Serve hot with rice or bread.

Pinto Beans, Mexican Style

Makes about 5 to 6 cups

2 cups dried pinto beans

2 medium-size yellow onions, chopped
1 small carrot, chopped
1 teaspoon finely chopped garlic
1 bay leaf
¼ cup vegetable oil (preferably cold-pressed safflower)

2 large ripe tomatoes, peeled, seeded and chopped, or ¼ cup tomato paste
2 teaspoons sea salt or 4 teaspoons coarse salt

Discard any discolored beans. Rinse remainder under cold running water. Drain well. Transfer to large bowl. Add enough cold water to allow beans to expand at least 2½ times, about 6 cups. Let soak at least 8 hours or overnight. (Beans can be quick-soaked: Boil 2 to 3 minutes. Remove from heat. Cover and soak 1 hour.)

    Transfer beans and soaking water to heavy large saucepan or Dutch oven. Add onion, carrot, garlic and bay leaf and bring to boil over medium-high heat. Reduce heat to low, cover tightly and simmer about 1 hour. Stir in oil, tomatoes and salt. Add more water if necessary; there should be enough liquid for a sauce, but it should not be soupy. Cover and continue cooking until beans are tender, about 30 minutes.

Frijoles Refritos

Makes about 5 to 6 cups

5 to 6 cups Pinto Beans, Mexican Style (see preceding recipe)
1 to 2 tablespoons vegetable oil, preferably cold-pressed safflower (optional)

  Seeded and chopped serrano chilies or jalapeño peppers or hot pepper sauce (optional)

Puree cooked beans in processor (not blender). If thicker consistency is desired, transfer to medium saucepan, stir in vegetable oil and cook uncovered over low heat, stirring occasionally until thick. Blend in chilies, peppers or several drops of hot pepper sauce.

Red Beans and Rice

8 to 10 servings

1 pound red beans
2 quarts water
1 meaty ham bone or 1 thick slice pork, cubed
1 pound hot sausage, thinly sliced
2 cups chopped onion
2 celery stalks, chopped
1 bunch green onions, chopped

1 green bell pepper, chopped
4 bay leaves
Pinch of thyme

Salt and freshly ground pepper
Hot pepper sauce
Freshly cooked rice

Rinse beans thoroughly; discard any bad ones. Place in Dutch oven and add water. Set over medium heat and add next 8 ingredients. Bring to boil, then reduce heat and simmer about 3 hours.

Using wooden spoon, mash about ⅓ to ½ of beans against side of pan (this gives a creamy smoothness characteristic of Creole red beans). Season with salt, pepper and hot sauce to taste. Serve over freshly cooked rice.

Green Beans

Green Beans with Tomato-Mushroom Sauce

8 to 10 servings

2 generous tablespoons dried wild (boletus) mushrooms* (do not substitute Chinese mushrooms)
½ cup hot water

3 tablespoons light-bodied olive oil
1 medium onion, minced
2 large garlic cloves, minced
1 16-ounce can plum tomatoes, seeded, drained and crushed

¼ cup tomato paste
¼ cup chicken stock
2½ teaspoons dried basil
2 teaspoons sugar
Salt and freshly ground pepper

2 pounds fresh green beans, trimmed and halved diagonally

Rinse mushrooms quickly under cold running water; drain well. Crumble into small bowl. Add hot water and let stand for 30 minutes.

Pour oil into medium nonaluminum skillet. Place over high heat until hot. Add onion and brown quickly. Add garlic and cook several seconds; *do not burn.* Add mushrooms and their liquid, tomatoes, tomato paste, stock and basil and blend well. Boil until thickened, about 5 minutes. Remove from heat and stir in sugar, salt and pepper. *(Can be prepared to this point several days ahead. Cover and refrigerate, or freeze several weeks.)*

Steam green beans until just crisp-tender, about 10 minutes. Rinse under cold running water to stop cooking process and retain color; drain well.

Transfer to medium skillet. Add sauce, tossing to coat and heat through. Turn into heated shallow bowl and serve immediately.

Beans can be prepared 1 day ahead and refrigerated. If stove-top space is at a premium, combine sauce and beans on large piece of foil, wrap securely and heat about 30 minutes in 350°F oven. Otherwise, just reheat in medium skillet over medium-high heat.

*Boletus mushrooms are available at Italian markets and specialty stores.

Fresh Green Bean and Tomato Salad

2 servings

½ pound fresh green beans, trimmed
2 tomatoes, peeled and quartered

Dressing
3 tablespoons olive oil
1 tablespoon Sherry wine vinegar
1 garlic clove, minced

1 teaspoon chopped fresh dill
1 teaspoon minced fresh parsley
¼ teaspoon Dijon mustard
Salt and freshly ground pepper

Cook beans in simmering salted water until crisp-tender, about 5 to 10 minutes. Drain well. Rinse under cold running water and drain again. Arrange on salad plates. Surround with tomato.

For dressing: Combine all ingredients in small bowl and whisk until blended. Pour over salad. Chill. Let stand at room temperature before serving.

Green Beans in Dill and Walnut Sauce

Depending on the garnish, this dish can be an accompaniment or a main course.

4 to 6 servings

1½ pounds fresh green beans, trimmed

¾ cup finely minced green onion
½ cup plus 1 tablespoon walnut oil
½ cup finely minced *fresh* dill (do not use dried dillweed)
¼ cup finely chopped fresh parsley (preferably Italian)
3 tablespoons cider vinegar

3 tablespoons coarsely chopped walnuts

½ cup finely cubed smoked ham (optional garnish)
½ cup finely cubed Gruyère cheese (optional garnish)
½ cup thinly sliced radishes (optional garnish)

Bring 3 quarts salted water to boil in large saucepan. Add beans and cook until just tender. Drain well and immediately run under cold water to stop cooking process. Drain again. Transfer to salad bowl and chill well.

Combine next 6 ingredients in blender and puree until smooth *(do not use processor or mixture will be too grainy)*. Pour over beans and toss well. Cover and chill at least 2 hours before serving.

Just before serving, garnish as desired.

Lemon-Pepper Green Beans

2 servings

½ pound fresh green beans, cut into 2-inch lengths

1 tablespoon butter
1 tablespoon minced fresh parsley

1 tablespoon fresh lemon juice
¼ cup diced red bell pepper *or* canned pimiento, drained
Salt and freshly ground pepper

Cook beans uncovered in rapidly boiling salted water to cover until crisp-tender, about 4 minutes. Drain; immediately immerse in bowl of ice water with a few ice cubes until cold to touch. Drain again just before reheating.

When ready to serve, combine butter, parsley and lemon juice in 10-inch skillet. Place over medium-high heat, add beans and toss until heated through. Stir in red pepper or pimiento and season with salt and pepper to taste.

Green Bean Fritters

6 servings

1 pound fresh green beans, trimmed
2 cups all purpose flour
2 teaspoons baking powder
1 teaspoon salt
½ teaspoon freshly grated nutmeg
¼ teaspoon freshly ground white pepper
1 to 1¼ cups milk
2 eggs, separated (room temperature)

¼ cup freshly grated Parmesan cheese
2 tablespoons finely minced onion
2 tablespoons chopped fresh parsley
2 tablespoons (¼ stick) butter, melted

Oil for deep frying
Freshly grated Parmesan cheese

Bring large amount of salted water to rapid boil over high heat. Meanwhile, cut beans into narrow julienne; cut julienne into 1-inch lengths. Add beans to boiling water and cook until just tender, about 5 to 7 minutes. Immediately drain beans and plunge into cold water to stop cooking process. Drain well; pat dry. *(Can be prepared up to 2 days ahead and refrigerated.)*

Sift flour, baking powder, salt, nutmeg and pepper into large bowl. Combine 1 cup milk and yolks in small bowl and whisk to blend. Add to flour mixture with ¼ cup Parmesan, onion, parsley and melted butter and mix well. If batter is too thick, stir in remaining ¼ cup milk 1 tablespoon at a time; fritter batter should not be runny.

Stir beans into batter. Beat egg whites in medium bowl until stiff but not dry. Heat oil in large saucepan or deep fryer to 375°F. Gently fold beaten egg whites into batter. Using 2 soup spoons, add batter to oil in batches and fry, turning once, until fritters are golden brown, about 2 to 3 minutes. Drain on paper towels. Sprinkle with additional Parmesan and serve.

Cheese and Green Bean Casserole

4 to 6 servings

4 tablespoons (½ stick) butter
1 onion, diced

2 tablespoons all purpose flour
1 teaspoon sugar
1 teaspoon salt
Freshly ground pepper

1 cup sour cream
¾ pound Swiss cheese, grated
4 cups frozen green beans, thawed
2 cups high protein wheat and rice cereal

Preheat oven to 400°F. Grease 2-quart baking dish. Melt 2 tablespoons butter in medium saucepan over medium heat. Add onion and sauté until tender, about 8 to 10 minutes. Remove onion from saucepan and set aside.

Melt remaining butter over low heat in same saucepan. Add flour, sugar, salt and pepper and mix thoroughly. Stir in sour cream and bring to boil. Cook, stirring constantly, until thickened, about 2 minutes. Add cheese, beans, cereal and reserved onion and mix well. Turn into prepared dish. Bake until cheese is melted, about 20 minutes. Serve hot.

Green Beans Provençal

4 servings

1½ pounds fresh green beans,
    trimmed

2 tablespoons olive oil
2 tablespoons fresh lemon juice

½ teaspoon minced garlic
½ teaspoon dried thyme, crumbled

½ lemon, thinly sliced (garnish)

Bring large pot of salted water to boil over high heat. Add beans and cook until just crisp-tender, about 4 minutes. Drain beans and rinse under cold water to stop cooking process; drain well and pat dry. *(Can be prepared ahead; set aside at room temperature.)*

    Heat olive oil in heavy large skillet over medium-high heat. Add beans and cook, stirring constantly, until heated through. Add lemon juice, garlic and thyme and cook 1 minute, tossing gently. Transfer to heated dish. Garnish with lemon slices and serve.

Braised Green Beans à la Basquaise

This spicy dish is extremely popular in the Basque region of northern Spain. It is traditionally served as an accompaniment to fried eggs and country sausage.

4 servings

1 pound small, narrow green beans

¼ cup imported olive oil
1 dried hot chili pepper, halved
5 to 6 tomatoes, peeled, seeded and
    chopped
¼ cup finely minced fresh parsley
3 large basil leaves, finely minced
2 garlic cloves, minced
1 large sprig fresh thyme or 1
    teaspoon dried

1 sprig fresh oregano or 1 teaspoon
    dried
Salt and freshly ground pepper

Minced parsley (garnish)

Freshly grated Parmesan cheese

Snap off ends of beans, leaving beans whole. Rinse under cold running water and drain well. Bring salted water to rolling boil in 6- to 8-quart pot. Add beans and cook 5 to 7 minutes until crisp-tender. Drain in colander and immediately plunge into ice water to stop cooking process. Set aside.

    Heat olive oil in heavy 8-inch iron skillet over high heat. Add chili pepper and cook until darkened. Discard pepper. Add tomatoes, parsley, basil, garlic, thyme, oregano, salt and pepper and bring to boil. Reduce heat, partially cover and simmer 20 to 25 minutes, until sauce is thick.

    Stir in green beans, cover and simmer an additional 10 minutes. Taste and correct seasonings. Garnish with minced parsley and serve directly from skillet. Pass Parmesan cheese separately.

    For a main course add 2 cups cooked white beans and some diced smoked ham or prosciutto. Add beans and ham to the thickened tomato sauce along with the green beans and simmer 15 minutes.

 # Corn

Peppery Corn and Cilantro Sauce

Delightful with grilled fish, chicken or pork. If a chunkier sauce is desired, do not strain the puree.

Makes about 1½ cups

1 to 1¼ cups whipping cream
¼ cup water
⅛ teaspoon minced garlic
⅛ teaspoon dried red pepper flakes or more to taste
2 cups fresh corn kernels (about 2 large or 4 small ears)

1½ tablespoons chopped fresh cilantro (also known as coriander or Chinese parsley)
Salt

Combine 1 cup cream, water, garlic and red pepper flakes in medium saucepan and bring to boil over medium heat. Reduce heat and simmer until reduced to 1 cup, about 10 minutes. Add corn and continue simmering until tender, about 5 to 8 minutes. Transfer to processor or blender and mix until smooth. Strain puree through very fine sieve set over clean saucepan. Place over medium heat and simmer 3 minutes to blend flavors, adding more cream if necessary. Stir in cilantro. Season with salt. Serve immediately.

Quick Old-Fashioned Corn Relish

Makes about 1⅔ cups

½ cup vinegar
⅓ cup sugar
1 teaspoon salt
½ teaspoon celery seed
¼ teaspoon mustard seed
¼ teaspoon hot pepper sauce

1½ cups cooked corn kernels or 16-ounce can whole kernel corn, drained

2 tablespoons chopped green bell pepper
1 tablespoon chopped pimiento
1 tablespoon minced white or green onion

Combine first 6 ingredients in medium saucepan and bring to boil. Cook 2 minutes; remove from heat and cool.

Place remaining ingredients in medium bowl. Add cooled mixture and blend lightly. Chill until serving.

This will keep indefinitely in the refrigerator; the flavor improves with standing.

Cream-Glazed Corn

2 servings

1 tablespoon butter
2 cups uncooked fresh corn kernels (about 2 large or 4 small ears) or frozen whole kernel corn, thawed
2 tablespoons water
Pinch of ground cloves

2 tablespoons whipping cream
Salt

Melt butter in small skillet over high heat. Immediately add corn, water and cloves. Cover and cook, stirring occasionally, 3 to 4 minutes. Add cream and stir constantly until cream is almost absorbed. Season with salt to taste.

Quick Corn Savories

Makes about 3 dozen small biscuits

6 tablespoons (¾ stick) butter
1½ cups buttermilk baking mix

1 8½-ounce can cream-style corn

Preheat oven to 400°F. Melt butter in 11 × 17-inch jelly roll pan. Combine baking mix and corn in medium bowl. Drop biscuits onto pan by heaping teaspoons. Turn in butter to coat well. Bake until golden, 20 minutes. Serve hot.

Roasted Corn with Garlic-Parmesan Spread

A new twist on a traditional favorite. Corn is roasted in the husk, then rolled in a fluffy garlic-Parmesan mayonnaise.

Makes about 2 cups

2 cups chicken stock
20 large garlic cloves, unpeeled

2 egg yolks, room temperature
2 teaspoons Dijon mustard
¼ teaspoon chopped garlic
　Juice of 1 lemon
　Dash of salt

1 cup oil, room temperature
½ cup freshly grated Parmesan cheese

Young corn in husk
Softened butter

Combine stock with garlic cloves in small saucepan and bring to boil. Let boil 10 minutes. Drain, reserving stock for another use. Rinse garlic under cold water and drain well. Slip off skins.

Transfer garlic to processor. Add yolks, mustard, chopped garlic, lemon juice and salt and mix until pale yellow and creamy. With machine running, gradually add oil through feed tube in thin steady stream, stopping machine occasionally to see if oil is absorbed. Add cheese and mix briefly just to combine.

Prepare fire and let coals burn down until just moderately hot.

Gently strip back husks from corn and remove silks. Rinse corn under cold water and pat dry with paper towels. Spread each ear with a bit of butter and then reassemble husk, twisting top to seal. Roast 20 minutes, turning often. Serve with Garlic-Parmesan Spread.

Spread can be prepared several days ahead and refrigerated. It can also be used as a dip for assorted raw vegetables.

Country Corn Pudding

4 to 6 servings

¼ cup (½ stick) butter
3 tablespoons all purpose flour
1½ cups milk or half and half

2 eggs
1 tablespoon chopped fresh parsley

1 teaspoon salt
¼ teaspoon ground red pepper
3 cups corn kernels
　Crumbled cooked bacon or cubed ham (optional)

Preheat oven to 350°F. Butter 2-quart baking dish. Melt butter in small skillet over medium-high heat. Add flour and stir until smooth. Cook 1 minute, stirring constantly. Gradually add milk, stirring constantly until sauce is thickened. Remove sauce from heat.

Beat eggs in large bowl. Gradually whisk sauce into eggs, blending well after each addition. Mix in parsley, salt and red pepper. Add corn and mix thoroughly. Turn into baking dish. Sprinkle top with bacon or ham. Bake until top is lightly golden and center is set, about 20 to 30 minutes.

Corn Pudding Soufflé in Cabbage with Sauce Nature

6 servings

6 large outer cabbage leaves

2 tablespoons (¼ stick) unsalted butter

3½ cups fresh corn kernels (4 to 6 large ears)

1 medium tomato, peeled, seeded and cut into ½-inch cubes

1 teaspoon minced fresh rosemary or ½ teaspoon dried, crumbled
Salt and freshly ground pepper

3 tablespoons unsalted butter

3 tablespoons all purpose flour

¾ cup milk

3 eggs, separated (room temperature)

Pinch of salt
Pinch of cream of tartar

Sauce Nature

1 medium tomato, peeled, seeded and coarsely chopped

1 cup crème fraîche or whipping cream

1 tablespoon chopped fresh marjoram or 1 teaspoon dried, crumbled

1 tablespoon snipped fresh chives

1 teaspoon chopped fresh dill or ½ teaspoon dried dillweed

Fresh marjoram, dill or parsley sprigs (garnish)

Bring large pot of salted water to rapid boil over high heat. Add cabbage leaves and cook until limp, about 2 minutes. Drain well; pat dry. Using small, sharp knife, pare down thick central vein on outer side of each leaf to same thickness as remainder of leaf.

Melt 2 tablespoons butter in large skillet over medium heat. Add corn, tomato, rosemary, salt and pepper and cook 5 minutes. Set aside.

Preheat oven to 425°F. Melt 3 tablespoons butter in medium saucepan over medium-low heat. Whisk in flour and let foam 3 minutes, stirring constantly. Whisk in milk. Increase heat to medium high and stir until mixture boils and thickens. Remove from heat. Whisk in egg yolks one at a time, blending thoroughly after each addition. Stir in corn mixture.

Beat egg whites with salt and cream of tartar in large bowl of electric mixer until stiff but not dry. Gently fold ¼ of whites into corn mixture, then fold corn mixture into remaining whites, being careful not to deflate. Taste and adjust seasoning as desired.

Generously butter six ½-cup ovenproof molds or ramekins. Fit 1 cabbage leaf into each mold to form cup. Spoon corn mixture evenly into cabbage leaves. Fold edges of leaves over corn (corn may not be completely covered). Cover each mold with round of buttered parchment paper. Arrange in deep baking dish. Pour enough simmering water into dish to come ¾ way up sides of molds. Bake until tops are golden and tester inserted in centers comes out clean, 20 to 25 minutes.

Meanwhile, prepare sauce: Puree tomato in processor or blender. Measure puree; return ½ cup to processor (reserve remaining puree for another use). Add all remaining ingredients except garnish and blend well.

Invert soufflés onto individual plates and surround with sauce. Top each with herb sprig. Serve immediately.

Indian Pudding

6 servings

2 cups milk
¼ cup cornmeal

¼ cup sugar
½ teaspoon salt
½ teaspoon ginger
½ teaspoon cinnamon

⅛ teaspoon baking soda
1 cup milk
¼ cup dark molasses

Whipped cream
Freshly grated nutmeg

Preheat oven to 275°F. In saucepan or top of double boiler, cook milk over low heat until hot. Add cornmeal a little at a time. Stirring constantly, cook 15 minutes or until mixture thickens. Remove from heat.

Mix together sugar, salt, ginger, cinnamon and baking soda in small bowl, then stir into cornmeal mixture. Add milk and molasses and blend thoroughly. Pour into 1-quart casserole and bake 2 hours.

Serve warm with whipped cream and a sprinkling of nutmeg.

Green Corn Tamales

6 to 8 servings

6 large ears of corn, including untrimmed husks

⅓ cup yellow cornmeal
1 3-ounce package cream cheese, room temperature
¼ cup butter, melted
3 tablespoons honey
1 egg, lightly beaten

1 teaspoon baking powder
1 teaspoon salt

½ cup tomato sauce
1 4-ounce can diced chilies, rinsed
1 cup coarsely grated Monterey Jack cheese

Cut through each corn cob at thickest part just above base. Unwrap husks very carefully, trying to keep them intact. Trim off points, rinse husks thoroughly and set aside to drain.

Remove silk from corn and cut kernels from cobs as near the core as possible (there should be 4 cups of kernels). Place corn kernels in blender or processor and puree briefly (texture should be rough, not smooth; with blender you may find it necessary to add up to ½ cup water to aid in pureeing). Place in heavy-bottomed saucepan. Add cornmeal, cream cheese, butter, honey, egg, baking powder and salt. Blend well.

Place over medium heat and cook until mixture has thickened to consistency of oatmeal, stirring constantly.

While mixture is cooking, bring large pan of water to boil. Dip husks into boiling water and heat until softened. Drain well.

Spread a thin coating of corn mixture (tamale dough) down middle of broadest part of husk, allowing for an overlap of about 1½ inches from broad part of husk and about 3 inches from pointed end. Spread tomato sauce down middle of tamale dough. Sprinkle with chilies and top with grated cheese.

Fold sides of husk together. Turn up pointed end of husk and fold broad end over it. Use narrow strips of husk, or string, for tying each tamale across top flap, or wrap in foil.

Place a layer of corn cobs in bottom of 8-quart stockpot. Add water to barely cover cobs. Place tamales on top of cobs, folded side up, cover and steam about

45 minutes. To test for doneness: Open husk. Filling should come easily away from husk, be spongy and well cooked throughout. Serve immediately.

Tamales may be prepared up to 1 week before serving and refrigerated. To reheat: If prepared in foil, place in double boiler or ungreased frying pan until warmed through. Remove foil and serve in husk. Without foil, place in steamer.

Tamales may also be frozen. Remove from freezer, wrap in foil (if not already in foil) and place in 350°F oven 30 minutes. Unwrap and serve.

🍒 Peas and Snow Peas

French Peas

6 to 8 servings

6 tablespoons butter
¼ cup finely chopped lettuce
1½ pounds frozen tiny peas, unthawed, or shelled fresh peas
¼ cup minced shallots or white part of green onion

1 large whole sprig parsley
2 to 4 teaspoons sugar
1 teaspoon salt
⅛ teaspoon white pepper

Melt butter in 3-quart saucepan. Place lettuce on top of butter. Add peas, shallots, parsley, sugar, salt and pepper. Simmer covered, stirring occasionally, 10 to 15 minutes, or until peas are just tender. Remove parsley before serving.

Stir-Fry of Fresh Fennel and Peas

For ease of preparation, slice and chop all ingredients a day ahead.

6 servings

4 to 5 small to medium fennel bulbs, cored and sliced into thin strips*
2 tablespoons fresh lemon juice
3 tablespoons olive oil
3 large shallots, minced
2 ounces boiled ham, diced
½ teaspoon fresh tarragon or ⅛ teaspoon dried, crumbled

1½ cups frozen tiny peas, thawed
2 green onions, cut into 1-inch lengths
2 tablespoons chopped fennel or celery leaves
Salt and freshly ground pepper

Combine fennel and lemon juice in medium bowl and let stand 10 minutes. Heat olive oil in wok or large skillet over high heat. Add fennel and shallot and stir-fry, tossing constantly, about 2 minutes. Remove from heat and add ham and tarragon. *(Can be prepared 1 hour ahead to this point.)*

About 5 minutes before serving, return mixture to high heat and toss until very hot. Add remaining ingredients and stir-fry just until heated through. Transfer to platter and serve.

Stir-fry leftovers can be used as a main dish. Transfer to greased shallow baking dish and sprinkle generously with shredded Gruyère or Parmesan cheese. Bake in 300°F oven until hot.

*One large bunch celery can be substituted. Separate into stalks. Cut in half crosswise, then slice thinly lengthwise.

Pea Soufflé Roll with Minted Vegetable Sauce

4 servings

2 tablespoons (¼ stick) unsalted butter
2 tablespoons minced shallot
1 cup shelled fresh peas (about 1 pound unshelled)
1 tablespoon minced fresh mint
  Pinch of sugar (optional)

4 ounces turnip, peeled and cut into ¼-inch dice (1 scant cup)
4 ounces boiling potato, peeled and cut into ¼-inch dice (¾ cup)
4 ounces fresh green beans, trimmed and cut into ¼-inch dice (1 scant cup)
1 large carrot, cut into ¼-inch dice (¾ cup)

Soufflé Roll
¼ cup (½ stick) unsalted butter
¼ cup all purpose flour
1⅓ cups milk
6 egg yolks, room temperature
3 tablespoons freshly grated Parmesan cheese
  Grated peel of 1 lemon

¾ teaspoon salt
¼ teaspoon freshly ground pepper
⅛ teaspoon freshly grated nutmeg
6 egg whites, room temperature
  Pinch of salt
  Pinch of cream of tartar

Minted Vegetable Sauce
4 egg yolks, room temperature
1 tablespoon fresh lemon juice
½ teaspoon salt
⅛ teaspoon white pepper
½ cup (1 stick) unsalted butter, heated to boiling

1 tablespoon unsalted butter
2 ounces minced prosciutto
2 to 3 teaspoons minced fresh mint
2 tablespoons whipping cream, lightly whipped

Mint sprigs (garnish)

Melt 2 tablespoons butter in heavy medium saucepan over medium-low heat. Add shallot and stir until translucent, about 2 minutes. Mix in peas and 1 tablespoon mint. Cover and cook until peas are tender, 12 to 15 minutes, stirring occasionally. Taste peas and add pinch of sugar if desired.

Bring large pot of salted water to rapid boil over high heat. Add turnip, potato, beans and carrot and cook until crisp-tender, 3 to 5 minutes. Drain vegetables well and pat dry. Set aside.

For roll: Preheat oven to 375°F. Line 11 × 16 × 1-inch jelly roll pan with aluminum foil or parchment paper, extending foil 1 inch beyond edge of pan. Generously butter foil and sprinkle with flour, shaking off excess. Melt butter in heavy medium saucepan over medium-low heat. Add flour and let foam, stirring, 3 minutes. Increase heat to medium high, pour in milk and cook, whisking constantly, until mixture boils and is very thick. Transfer to processor or blender in batches. Add pea mixture and coarsely puree using on/off turns. With machine running, add yolks one at a time and mix until smooth puree, stopping as necessary to scrape down sides of work bowl. (For finer texture, strain soufflé mixture through fine sieve.) Blend in Parmesan, lemon peel, salt, pepper and nutmeg. Beat whites with salt and cream of tartar in large bowl of electric mixer until stiff but not dry. Gently fold in puree. Spread evenly in prepared pan using rubber spatula. Bake until soufflé is puffed and softly set, about 18 to 20 minutes.

Meanwhile, prepare sauce: Combine egg yolks, lemon juice, salt and pepper in processor or blender and mix until smooth, 5 to 8 seconds. With machine running, pour in boiling butter a drop at a time. Turn off machine as soon as all butter has been added.

Melt 1 tablespoon butter in heavy medium saucepan over medium-high heat. Add cooked vegetables and stir just until heated through, about 1 minute; *do not overcook*. Remove from heat. Stir in yolk mixture, prosciutto and mint. Fold in cream. Taste and season with salt and white pepper.

Remove soufflé roll from oven. Dampen nonterry kitchen towel with hot water and wring dry. Pull tautly over pan. Top with board or baking sheet. Turn pan over, letting roll invert onto towel; peel off aluminum foil. Spread vegetable sauce evenly over soufflé, leaving ¼-inch border on all sides. Using towel as aid, roll soufflé up lengthwise. Transfer to heated platter seam side down. Garnish with mint sprigs and serve.

Leftover soufflé can be served cold or hot. To reheat, cover with aluminum foil and warm in 400°F oven for about 10 minutes.

Steamed Snow Peas with Nutmeg à la Façon de Déjà-Vu

4 servings

⅓ pound fresh snow peas

1 tablespoon clarified butter

Freshly grated nutmeg
Salt and freshly ground pepper

Bring 6 cups water to boil in medium saucepan over medium heat. Set snow peas in steamer or strainer above water and steam 1 minute. Drain well.

Heat butter in medium skillet over medium-high heat. Add snow peas and sauté until tender, about 1 to 2 minutes. Season with nutmeg, salt and pepper to taste. Serve immediately.

Sesame Snow Peas with Red Pepper

4 servings

1 teaspoon vegetable oil
2 cups fresh snow peas, strings removed
1 large red bell pepper, seeded, and cut into very thin julienne*

1 teaspoon sesame oil**
2 teaspoons toasted sesame seed

Combine 1 teaspoon vegetable oil and enough water to cover peas and pepper in heavy saucepan. Bring to boil over high heat. Add peas and red pepper and cook until crisp-tender, 3 to 5 minutes. Drain immediately. Transfer to bowl. Add sesame oil and toss gently. Sprinkle with sesame and serve.

*An equal amount of roasted red bell peppers can be substituted. Add peppers to peas with sesame oil and toss gently.
** Available in oriental markets.

Braised Peas in Avocado Cups

8 servings

¼ cup (½ stick) unsalted butter
4 shallots, minced
1 leek (white part only), minced
12 ounces shelled fresh peas or 12 ounces frozen tiny peas, thawed
3 tablespoons rich chicken stock
1½ to 2 teaspoons sugar
4 Boston lettuce leaves, chopped

Salt and freshly ground pepper

1 cup sour cream
¾ cup freshly grated Parmesan cheese
4 avocados, halved and seeded, some pulp scooped out
Juice of 2 lemons

Preheat oven to 375°F. Melt butter in 3-quart saucepan over medium heat. Add shallots and leek, cover and cook until shallots are softened, about 5 minutes.

Add peas, chicken stock, sugar and lettuce. Cover and cook until peas are tender, about 10 minutes (if using frozen peas cook only until heated through). Season with salt and pepper.

Combine sour cream with Parmesan. Arrange avocado halves on baking sheet and sprinkle generously with lemon juice. Divide peas among halves and top with sour cream. Bake until heated through, about 10 minutes.

Sugar Snap Peas with Mushrooms

2 servings

1 tablespoon oil
3 mushrooms, sliced
⅛ pound fresh sugar snap peas,*
   fresh snow peas or thawed frozen
   snow peas, cut into half crosswise

1 teaspoon soy sauce
1 to 2 tablespoons toasted sesame
   seed

Heat oil in wok or large skillet over medium-high heat. Add mushrooms and stir-fry until lightly browned. Reduce heat to medium, cover and simmer 3 minutes. Increase heat, add peas and stir-fry until crisp-tender, about 2 minutes. Stir in soy sauce. Cover and cook 1 minute longer. Sprinkle with sesame seed and serve.

*If using sugar snap peas, remove string by gripping it firmly at tip and pulling along straight side of pea toward stem. Pinch off stem and discard. Continue pulling string until it is completely removed.

Snow Peas and Tomatoes

4 servings

2 to 3 tablespoons butter
1 garlic clove, minced
¼ cup finely chopped onion
2 7-ounce packages frozen snow
   peas, thawed
1 8-ounce can water chestnuts,
   drained and sliced

1 tablespoon soy sauce
1 teaspoon salt
1 teaspoon dried oregano leaves,
   crumbled
3 medium tomatoes, cut into
   ¼-inch dice

Melt butter with garlic in large skillet over medium heat. Add onion and sauté until crisp-tender, about 1 minute. Blend in remaining ingredients except tomatoes and cook, stirring constantly, about 2 to 3 minutes. Stir in tomatoes and continue cooking until heated through, about 2 to 3 minutes. Serve hot.

4 🍎 Squash

No collection of vegetables would be complete without a mention of squash—cucumbers, christophenes, pattypan, pumpkin and zucchini. These are some of the most popular vegetables, as well as the most readily available. Any home gardener who has ever stood on a dusty patch of ground only to see it yield, almost instantly, large quantities of squash—especially zucchini—will attest to this family's hardy nature. And any cook will attest to the delicious flavor and adaptability of these vegetables.

Squash is also a master of disguise. Crisp, crunchy and with a delectable assertive flavor in its natural state, it becomes soft and delicate with cooking. For instance, enjoy the freshness of Zesty Cucumber Salad or Sunomono, then contrast that with dill-enhanced Sautéed Cucumbers (page 50) and discover how one vegetable can take on an entirely different texture when cooked. Pickle lovers will want to try small cucumbers in a whole new guise: mellowed with cider vinegar, mustard, curry powder, turmeric and ground red pepper (page 51), a combination ideal as an accompaniment to roast lamb, pork or chicken.

Acorn squash, with a texture similar to pumpkin, can be used in many recipes in place of it—pies included. Here we present acorn squash in a delectable side dish "cup" for small onions laced with Sherry (page 58) or mixed with risotto (page 59) for a unique pasta course.

Zucchini is included in a selection of dishes that highlights its versatility: everything from a salad with green pepper, celery and onion accented with Burgundy (page 51) to terrific specialties with an Italian flair—Zucchini Pizza (where the vegetable provides the crust, page 53), Zucchini Lasagna with Caciocavallo (page 54), and Zucchini with Pesto (page 52).

These savory main courses and accompaniments are perfect ways to showcase some timeless favorites. You will find them winners for brunch, lunch and dinner.

 Cucumbers

Zesty Cucumber Salad

Whether you call it a salad or a relish, this is an excellent accompaniment for chicken.

6 servings

4 large cucumbers, peeled, halved lengthwise and seeded
2 teaspoons salt

2 small white onions, halved and thinly sliced

½ cup distilled white vinegar
2 teaspoons Hungarian sweet paprika
1 teaspoon sugar or to taste

Slice cucumbers as thinly as possible. Transfer to large bowl. Sprinkle with salt and toss lightly. Cover with plastic wrap and refrigerate overnight.

Drain cucumber; squeeze dry. Combine all remaining ingredients in medium bowl. Stir in cucumber. Cover and chill thoroughly before serving.

Sunomono

6 servings

1 large cucumber, lightly peeled and thinly sliced
¾ teaspoon salt

¾ cup cider vinegar

½ cup sugar
Lettuce leaves (optional)

Tomato slices, crabmeat and tiny shrimp (garnish)

Sprinkle cucumber slices with salt. Allow to stand at room temperature 1 hour. Gently squeeze slices until soft and pliable.

Combine vinegar and sugar in small bowl, stirring until sugar dissolves. Add about half of vinegar mixture to cucumber and toss lightly; drain. Just before serving pour remaining vinegar mixture over cucumber. Divide among individual small bowls or spoon onto lettuce leaves and garnish with sliced tomatoes, crabmeat and shrimp.

Sautéed Cucumbers

4 servings

2 large cucumbers, peeled, seeded and cut julienne
2 teaspoons salt

1 cup whipping cream
2 tablespoons chopped fresh dill

Freshly ground pepper

2 tablespoons (¼ stick) butter

Toss cucumber with salt in colander and let drain 20 minutes. Rinse under cold running water and let drain again. Pat dry with paper towel. Meanwhile, boil cream, dill and pepper in small saucepan until mixture is reduced by half, about 20 minutes. Set aside.

Melt butter in large skillet over medium-high heat. Add cucumber and sauté until crisp-tender, about 3 to 5 minutes. Stir in cream mixture. Cook until heated through, about 2 to 3 minutes. Serve immediately.

Curry Pickles

For best flavor, age pickles for three months before opening. Excellent with cold pork, chicken or roast lamb.

Makes about 3½ quarts

8 pounds slender small cucumbers, well scrubbed

2½ quarts cider vinegar
⅓ cup sugar
⅓ cup coarse salt
⅓ cup dry mustard

⅓ cup curry powder
⅓ cup pickling spice
¼ cup mustard seed
1½ teaspoons ground turmeric
½ teaspoon ground red pepper

Bring large amount of water to boil in stockpot over high heat. Meanwhile, trim all stems and blossoms from cucumbers, discarding any cucumbers that are soft. Add cucumbers to boiling water and blanch 30 seconds. Drain well; pat dry. Pack tightly into clean, hot jars to ½ inch from top.

Combine remaining ingredients in stockpot and bring to rapid boil. Ladle enough hot brine into 1 jar just to cover cucumbers. Run plastic knife or spatula between cucumbers and jar to release any air bubbles. Clean rim and threads of jar with damp cloth. Seal jar with new, scalded, very hot lid. Repeat with remaining jars. Transfer jars to gently simmering (180°F to 190°F) water bath and process for 10 minutes. Let jars cool on rack. Test for seal. Store pickles in cool dry place.

 *Zucchini*

Zucchini Salad

6 servings

3 medium zucchini, thinly sliced
⅔ cup cider vinegar
½ cup shredded green bell pepper
½ cup shredded celery
½ cup shredded yellow onion
½ cup sugar

⅓ cup oil
¼ cup Burgundy
2 tablespoons red wine vinegar
1 teaspoon salt
½ teaspoon freshly ground pepper

Combine all ingredients in large bowl and mix thoroughly. Cover and refrigerate at least 6 hours before serving.
Salad will keep up to 2 weeks.

Zucchini Cheese Salad

2 servings

¼ cup sour cream or plain yogurt
½ teaspoon Dijon mustard
½ teaspoon prepared horseradish
Pinch of ground cumin
Salt and freshly ground pepper
¼ pound Swiss cheese, cut julienne

1 zucchini, grated and drained
4 mushrooms, thinly sliced
½ cup sliced celery
Lettuce leaves

2 radishes, grated (garnish)

Combine first 4 ingredients with salt and pepper to taste. Place cheese, zucchini, mushrooms and celery in bowl and toss gently with sour cream dressing. Spoon onto lettuce leaves and sprinkle with grated radish.

Zucchini Spaghetti with Chive Sauce
(Spaghettis de Courgettes à la Ciboulette)

This recipe is an adaptation of a dish created by Guy Tricon and Jean André, the brilliant young chef-owners of Restaurant Mourrachonne. They serve it as a first course — a small mound of zucchini "pasta" bracketed by chive sauce and fresh tomato-basil sauce. Use the julienne disc of a processor or a fine grater to shred the zucchini.

4 servings

3 pounds zucchini, peeled and shredded (about 4 inches long)
Salt

Chive Sauce
2 tablespoons (¼ stick) butter
6 medium shallots, finely chopped
2 medium leeks, well washed and finely chopped
1 small celery stalk, finely chopped
1 very small carrot, finely chopped
½ cup dry white wine
1 bay leaf

¼ teaspoon dried thyme, crumbled
2 cups half and half
Salt and freshly ground white pepper
¼ cup freshly snipped chives
Juice of ½ lemon

2 tablespoons (¼ stick) unsalted butter
Freshly ground pepper
Tomato-basil sauce (optional; use your favorite recipe)

Spread zucchini in single layer on paper towels. Sprinkle generously with salt. Top with more paper towels. Weight with heavy object and let stand 2 to 3 hours to remove excess liquid.

For sauce: Melt 2 tablespoons butter in heavy medium skillet over medium-low heat. Add shallot, leek, celery and carrot and cook 10 minutes, stirring frequently; *do not brown.* Add wine, bay leaf and thyme. Increase heat to high and boil until wine is reduced to 2 tablespoons, about 10 minutes. Stir in half and half and continue boiling until reduced by half, about 5 minutes. Remove from heat and discard bay leaf. Transfer mixture to processor or blender and puree. Return to pan. Season with salt and white pepper to taste. Blend in chives and lemon juice. Set sauce aside and keep warm.

Melt butter in large skillet over medium heat. Add zucchini and cook until crisp-tender, stirring frequently, about 2 minutes. Season with salt and pepper to taste. Just before serving, divide zucchini into fourths, twirl each portion around fork and mound in center of plates. Surround with chive sauce; or spoon chive sauce to one side of zucchini and tomato-basil sauce to the other.

Zucchini with Pesto

4 to 6 servings

Pesto Sauce
¼ cup freshly grated Parmesan cheese
¼ cup olive oil
3 tablespoons coarsely chopped fresh basil or 1 tablespoon dried, crumbled
1 garlic clove

Saltato
2 tablespoons olive oil
3 medium zucchini, cubed
1 onion, minced
3 medium tomatoes, cubed
1 teaspoon salt

Parsley sprig (garnish)

For sauce: Combine all ingredients in processor or blender and mix well. (Or mash basil with garlic using mortar and pestle. Add Parmesan cheese and oil and work into a paste.)

For saltato: Place large skillet over high heat until very hot, about 30 seconds. Add oil, coating bottom evenly. Add zucchini and onion and continue stirring 3 minutes. Add tomatoes and salt and stir-fry an additional minute. Remove from heat and blend in Pesto Sauce, stirring briskly until thoroughly mixed. Turn onto heated platter and garnish with parsley sprig. Serve immediately.

Zucchini Pizza

4 to 6 servings

3 cups grated zucchini
3 eggs, well beaten
⅓ cup all purpose flour
¼ teaspoon salt

2 cups grated mozzarella cheese
1 2¼-ounce can sliced black olives, drained
⅔ cup minced green onion

½ cup minced Italian pickled peppers
1 teaspoon dried oregano
½ teaspoon dried basil
3 medium tomatoes, thinly sliced
Salt

Preheat oven to 450°F. Generously grease pizza pan, 9 × 13-inch baking dish, or baking sheet with rim. Press excess liquid from zucchini. Transfer pulp to mixing bowl. Add eggs, flour and salt and blend well. Spread evenly in prepared pan and bake 8 minutes. Remove from oven and reduce temperature to 350°F.

Cover zucchini with cheese. Combine next 3 ingredients and sprinkle evenly over cheese. Top with oregano and basil. Arrange tomato slices over top and sprinkle very lightly with salt. Bake until base is set, about 20 minutes.

Baked Curried Zucchini

4 to 6 servings

1 egg
1 cup all purpose flour
1 teaspoon salt
1 teaspoon curry powder
¼ teaspoon freshly ground pepper

3 medium zucchini, cut into ¼-inch slices
Olive oil
Additional curry powder (optional)

Preheat oven to 400°F. Generously grease baking sheet. Beat egg well in small bowl and set aside. Combine flour, salt, curry powder and pepper in shallow dish. Dip zucchini in egg, then roll in seasoned flour, covering completely. Arrange zucchini on prepared sheet. Sprinkle zucchini generously with olive oil and additional curry powder, if desired. Bake until crisp and golden brown, turning once, about 20 minutes. Drain any excess liquid and serve immediately.

Zucchini Bake

6 to 8 servings

1 cup shredded sharp cheddar cheese
½ cup cottage cheese
4 eggs, beaten
3 tablespoons minced fresh parsley
1½ teaspoons salt
¼ teaspoon freshly ground pepper

2 pounds zucchini, sliced into ¼-inch rounds
¾ cup breadcrumbs
¼ cup grated Parmesan cheese
¼ cup (½ stick) butter

Preheat oven to 375°F. Butter inside of shallow 2-quart baking dish. Combine first 6 ingredients in bowl and mix well. Place layer of zucchini in baking dish and layer with some of cheese mixture. Repeat, ending with cheese mixture. Combine breadcrumbs and Parmesan in small bowl. Sprinkle over casserole. Dot with butter. Tent with foil and bake 25 minutes. Remove foil and bake an additional 20 minutes, until top is browned.
Must be assembled just before baking.

Baked Zucchini Frittata

6 *servings*

¾ tablespoon olive oil
3 cups thinly sliced zucchini
4 green onions, minced
3 tablespoons minced fresh parsley
8 eggs

⅔ cup freshly grated Romano cheese
1 teaspoon oregano
¼ teaspoon salt
   Dash of freshly ground pepper

Preheat oven to 350°F. Lightly grease 9-inch square baking pan. Heat oil in large skillet over medium heat. Add zucchini, onion and parsley and sauté until softened, about 4 to 5 minutes. Remove from heat and set aside. In large bowl, beat eggs with cheese and seasonings. Add zucchini mixture and blend well. Pour into prepared pan and bake until just firm in center, about 20 to 25 minutes. Serve hot or cold.

Zucchini Lasagne with Caciocavallo Cheese

2 *servings*

Sauce
3 tablespoons olive oil
½ cup finely chopped onion
1 celery stalk, finely chopped
1 garlic clove, finely chopped
1 pound fresh tomatoes, chopped, or 1 1-pound can whole tomatoes, drained and chopped
2 tablespoons minced fresh parsley
1 tablespoon tomato paste
1 tablespoon minced fresh basil or 1 teaspoon dried, crumbled
   Salt and freshly ground pepper

Filling
2 tablespoons (¼ stick) butter

1 small zucchini (about ¼ pound), cut into ¼-inch slices
¼ pound mushrooms, cleaned, stemmed and cut into ¼-inch slices
¼ cup whipping cream
2 tablespoons freshly grated Parmesan cheese

2 lasagne noodles
4 ounces caciocavallo cheese, coarsely grated (provolone can be substituted)
¼ cup freshly grated Parmesan or Romano cheese

For sauce: Heat olive oil in large skillet over medium heat. Add onion, celery and garlic and cook until softened, about 5 minutes. Stir in tomatoes, parsley, tomato paste and basil and simmer 20 to 25 minutes, breaking up tomatoes as sauce cooks. Puree sauce in food mill or by pressing through strainer. Season to taste with salt and pepper *(be careful; caciocavallo can be salty).*

For filling: Melt butter in small skillet over high heat. Add zucchini and mushrooms and sauté until lightly browned around edges. Stir in cream and continue cooking until cream is reduced to smooth, syrupy consistency. Let cool. Blend in 2 tablespoons Parmesan. Season with salt and pepper.

Bring large saucepan of salted water to rapid boil over high heat. Add noodles and cook just until tender, about 10 to 15 minutes. Drain well; pat dry with paper towels. Cut noodles in half crosswise. Cover bottoms of 2 individual gratin dishes with thin layer of tomato sauce. Lay 1 piece of noodle in each dish, trimming or tucking in any excess. Spoon ¼ of filling over each. Sprinkle with half of caciocavallo. Repeat layers of tomato sauce, pasta, filling and cheese. Top with remaining tomato sauce. Sprinkle with grated Parmesan or Romano. *(Can be prepared ahead to this point, covered tightly with foil or plastic and refrigerated or frozen. Bring to room temperature before baking.)*

Preheat oven to 450°F. Bake until lasagne is bubbly and cheese is lightly browned, about 10 to 15 minutes. Let stand 5 minutes before serving.

Bulgur Zucchini Casserole

6 to 8 servings

3 tablespoons butter
1 cup bulgur
½ cup minced onion
2 cups beef or chicken stock
1 teaspoon dried oregano, crumbled
½ teaspoon dried basil, crumbled

1 8-ounce can tomato sauce
½ pound zucchini, thinly sliced
1 cup cottage cheese
½ cup grated Parmesan cheese

Grease 2-quart heatproof baking dish. Melt butter in large skillet over medium-high heat. Add bulgur and onion and sauté until onion is tender, about 10 minutes. Blend in stock, oregano and basil. Cover and bring to boil. Reduce heat and simmer until liquid is absorbed, about 15 minutes.

Stir in tomato sauce and zucchini. Cover and simmer, stirring occasionally, until zucchini is crisp-tender, about 15 to 20 minutes. Turn into baking dish. Spoon cottage cheese evenly over bulgur mixture. Sprinkle Parmesan over top. Broil 4 inches from heat source until top is lightly brown, about 3 to 5 minutes. Serve immediately.

Stuffed Zucchini

2 servings

2 medium zucchini
½ cup grated cheddar cheese
1 tablespoon chopped green chilies
½ tomato, peeled, seeded and diced
Salt

Flour
1 to 2 eggs, lightly beaten

Oil for deep frying

Cook zucchini in boiling salted water for 5 minutes. Plunge immediately into cold water to stop cooking process.

Using small sharp knife or apple corer, hollow out zucchini lengthwise through center. Mix cheese, chilies, tomato and salt in small bowl. Pack into centers of zucchini. Roll zucchini in flour and then in beaten egg.

Heat oil in heavy skillet or deep fryer to 365°F. Fry zucchini until coating is crisp and cheese has begun to melt. Remove with slotted spoon and drain on paper towels. Serve hot.

Can be prepared ahead and kept warm in 200°F oven for 15 to 20 minutes.

🍎 Stuffed Vegetables

The very best vegetables are those picked in their infancy, tiny, tender and still glistening with the fresh dew of morning. But as summer wears on, the garden patch seems to explode, producing faster than it can be harvested. When you encounter the inevitable zucchini that has grown to the size of a Volkswagen, you can turn a liability into an asset with wonderful stuffed vegetable dishes.

Even those who don't raise their own will need to find uses for mature vegetables, since many farmers, choosing heft over flavor, wait to pick their crops until they have reached maximum growth. As a result, by the end of summer, markets and kitchen gardens alike are flooded with oversized vegetables that are perfect for stuffing.

Few dishes offer greater possibilities for experiment and improvisation. Be adventurous and try your own combinations, or take a filling from one recipe and use it in another.

Vegetables most adapted to stuffing are artichokes, cabbage, tomatoes, zucchini, peppers, onions, turnips, mushrooms and eggplant. Many of these can be filled, cooked and served either hot or cold. Tomatoes and mushrooms, may be stuffed and served without any cooking whatsoever.

Cabbage: This international favorite comes in three basic types. The most common variety is the green, smooth-headed cabbage, excellent for stuffing. Equally good for this purpose is the elegant frilly-leafed savoy. The purple cabbage is usually used for salads. When choosing any cabbage, select a head that is firm and solid, one that has unblemished outer leaves.

Artichoke: These graceful globes make attractive receptacles for a number of hot or cold mixtures. In the most popular presentation, the choke is removed and the center is stuffed with anything from rice to shrimp. For a variation, fill the center, then tuck tiny bits of stuffing in between the leaves. Stuffed artichokes should be set on a rack in a kettle over a small amount of

Italian Stuffed Zucchini

The filling amount can be increased for stuffing even larger squash. Bigger zucchini will need to cook longer; just keep testing them with knife tip until they feel tender.

4 servings

2 10-inch-long zucchini (about 1¼ pounds)

4 Italian sausages
1 onion, chopped
1 garlic clove, minced

1 cup uncooked small shell macaroni

1 tomato, peeled, seeded and chopped

1 cup grated cheddar cheese
2 tablespoons minced fresh parsley
1 teaspoon dried oregano
Salt and freshly ground pepper

2 tablespoons olive oil

¼ cup freshly grated Parmesan cheese

Cut zucchini in half lengthwise. Hollow out each half, leaving shell ¼ to ½ inch thick. Chop pulp; measure 2 cups (use remainder in other recipes).

simmering water; cover and steam over low heat for 30 to 40 minutes or until done. Serve hot, cold or at room temperature. When buying, choose tight, compact globes that are heavy for their size.

Summer squash: Zucchini, crookneck and pattypan squash, because of their delicate flavors, are ideal for stuffing, but fillings should not overwhelm. Season with tarragon, parsley and sautéed shallot and onion.

Pepper: Because of their assertive flavor, peppers should be stuffed with well-seasoned mixtures that have some flavor authority of their own. Italian sausage or any ground meat is a good complement. Choose sweet green or red bell peppers, glossy and firm and without blemishes. Buy just before using, since it is difficult to provide them with the 45- to 50-degree temperature and 90 percent humidity they need for long-term storage. (Hot peppers can also be stuffed with great success.)

Tomato: Tomatoes make attractive containers for any number of cold salad mixtures, or they can be filled with meat combinations and baked for a hot dish. When baking tomatoes, it's a good idea to put a teaspoon or two of raw rice in the shell before adding the filling. Rice absorbs the juices from the tomatoes and prevents stuffing from becoming soggy.

Eggplant: In Europe, where it's known as *aubergine,* this purple beauty forms the base for any number of spectacular dishes. Seek out eggplants with sleek, shiny exteriors—no wrinkles or brown spots. The flesh should be firm and slightly resistant to pressure.

Onion: Although they are indispensable in the kitchen, onions are often overlooked in their own right. Serve translucent baked onions with a savory filling to accompany roasts, steaks or broiled chicken. Serve them cold as an appetizer. Be sure to parboil onions for 10 minutes before stuffing, or they will take forever to cook and could burst.

Remove sausage from casings. Cook in skillet over medium heat, crumbling meat as it cooks. When sausage has rendered some of its fat, add zucchini pulp, onion and garlic and continue cooking until onion is soft and sausage has lost all of its pink color.

Meanwhile cook macaroni in pot of rapidly boiling water until al dente, about 5 minutes. Drain in colander.

Preheat oven to 350°F. Drain fat from sausage. Combine sausage with macaroni, tomato, cheddar cheese, parsley, oregano, salt and pepper; blend well.

Brush insides of zucchini halves with oil. Mound filling in halves and place in shallow baking dish. Add about ½ inch hot water to dish. Cover with foil and bake until zucchini are tender when pierced with knife tip, about 30 minutes. Remove from oven; discard foil.

Preheat broiler. Drain any water remaining in dish (a bulb baster works well). Sprinkle halves with Parmesan and run under broiler until cheese is light golden brown and bubbly.

Miscellaneous Squash

Betty's Summer Squash

6 to 8 servings

1 pound pattypan squash, cooked, chopped and drained thoroughly
4 eggs, beaten
2 cups milk

10 soda crackers, crumbled
Salt and freshly ground pepper
1 cup grated sharp cheddar cheese

Preheat oven to 325°F. Generously butter 6-cup baking dish 3 inches deep. Combine all ingredients except cheese in large bowl and mix well. Transfer to prepared dish. Sprinkle with cheese. Bake until mixture is bubbly, approximately 40 minutes. Serve immediately.

Chili-Stuffed Pattypan Squash

This pretty green scallop-edged squash filled with a creamy chili mixture is a great treat when served with any grilled or barbecued meat.

8 servings

2 tablespoons (¼ stick) butter

8 pattypan squash
8 ounces cream cheese, room temperature
3 tablespoons chopped green chilies

2 tablespoons half and half
Salt and freshly ground pepper
Dash of hot pepper sauce

¼ cup grated Monterey Jack cheese

Preheat oven to 400°F. Place butter in baking dish and set in oven until butter has melted. Remove from oven.

Trim ends of squash and scoop out centers, leaving firm shell. Combine cream cheese, chilies, half and half, salt and pepper and hot pepper sauce in small bowl and beat until well blended. Spoon into squash. Place squash in baking dish and cover with foil. Bake until tender, about 1 hour. Remove from oven.

Preheat broiler. Discard foil from baking dish and sprinkle squash with cheese. Run under broiler until cheese is golden brown and bubbly.

Acorn Squash with Sherried Onions

6 servings

3 small acorn squash
Melted butter
Salt

2 pounds peeled small white boiling onions

3 tablespoons butter
2 tablespoons dry Sherry
Salt and pepper
Chopped fresh parsley

Preheat oven to 400°F. Wash squash; cut in half crosswise and remove seeds. Brush cut surfaces of each half with melted butter. Place cut side down in shallow baking dish. Bake 30 minutes. Turn cut side up, sprinkle with salt and bake 25 to 30 minutes more, until squash is tender.

While squash is baking, simmer onions, covered, in lightly salted water about 20 minutes, or until tender. Drain well.

Melt 3 tablespoons butter in large skillet. Sauté onions, turning to brown on all sides. Add Sherry and cook 3 to 5 minutes. Season with salt and pepper. Fill acorn halves with sautéed onions. Sprinkle with chopped parsley.

Risotto with Pumpkin or Acorn Squash

2 servings

1 tablespoon butter
¼ cup finely chopped onion
4 ounces fresh pumpkin or acorn squash, peeled, seeded and cut into ⅛-inch cubes (1 cup)
1½ cups hot chicken stock (preferably homemade)
½ cup Arborio rice*
 Salt and freshly ground white pepper

Pinch of freshly grated nutmeg (optional)
3 tablespoons freshly grated Parmesan cheese

Additional freshly grated Parmesan cheese (garnish)

Melt butter in medium saucepan over medium heat. Add onion and cook until translucent but not browned, about 5 to 8 minutes. Stir in pumpkin or squash. Add just enough hot stock to cover (about ½ cup). Cook, stirring occasionally, 10 minutes. Stir in rice and just enough additional stock to cover and continue cooking, stirring occasionally until liquid evaporates. Add remaining stock a little at a time stirring until rice is tender but still al dente, about 15 to 20 minutes. Season to taste with salt, white pepper and nutmeg. Stir in 3 tablespoons cheese. Turn into dish. Sprinkle with additional cheese and serve.

*Arborio rice, the short-grained variety best suited for risotto, is available at Italian and specialty food stores. If you can't find it, California pearl rice is a good substitute.

Succulent Squash Bake

8 servings

2 pounds crookneck squash, cut into ½-inch slices
2 tablespoons dehydrated minced onion
2 cups grated cheddar cheese
1 10-ounce can chopped tomatoes and green chilies, drained

¾ cup (1½ sticks) butter
 Salt and freshly ground pepper
1½ cups cracker crumbs

Preheat oven to 350°F. Butter 2-quart baking dish. Combine squash and onion in large saucepan with enough salted water to cover. Cook over medium heat until squash is crisp-tender, about 5 to 7 minutes. Drain thoroughly.

   Transfer to bowl. Add cheese, tomatoes and chilies, ½ cup butter and salt and pepper and toss gently to blend. Transfer to prepared dish. Melt remaining ¼ cup butter in small saucepan. Pour over squash mixture. Sprinkle evenly with cracker crumbs. Bake until bubbly and heated through, about 30 minutes.

   This dish freezes well.

Stuffed Christophenes

6 servings

3 large christophenes,* washed
  and halved lengthwise
½ cup (1 stick) butter
1 medium onion, minced
  Celery salt
  Seasoned salt

Salt and freshly ground pepper
1 cup grated cheddar cheese
½ cup plus 2 tablespoons fine dry
  breadcrumbs
  Freshly grated Parmesan cheese

Preheat oven to 350°F. Bring enough salted water to cover christophenes to boil over medium-high heat. Add christophenes and cook until almost tender, about 20 minutes. Drain and cool.

Discard seeds. Scoop pulp into medium bowl (set shells aside). Add butter and onion to pulp with celery salt and seasoned salt to taste and mash well. Taste and season with salt and pepper. Fold in cheddar and ½ cup breadcrumbs. Fill shells evenly with stuffing. Top with remaining breadcrumbs. Sprinkle lightly with Parmesan. Bake until lightly browned, about 15 minutes. Arrange on large platter.

*This tropical squash, also called chayote or vegetable pear, is available in Latin American and specialty food markets.

5 ❦ Vegetable-Fruits

Although they bear no resemblance to oranges, bananas or berries, the vegetables in this chapter are actually all fruits. And while it is unlikely any of them will turn up on the dessert cart, they offer an infinite number of possibilities for delicious appetizers, main courses and accompaniments.

Eggplant is important in the provincial dishes of France and Italy, but you are just as likely to find it in many Mediterranean and Middle Eastern recipes. We offer a delightful cross-section here, including Eggplant Cream (page 63), Eggplant Custards (page 66) and Arabic Eggplant Eggah (page 68). Eggplant "Crepes" Sorrento (page 70) is a hearty do-ahead entrée in which the vegetable is used as a wrapper for an herbed mushroom-cheese filling—a terrific party dish.

Avocados have become abundant across the country and are favored for their smooth, creamy pulp. The two versions here—Avocado Mousse and Avocado Tempura with Nuts and Cheese (both page 62)—showcase its versatility and flavor.

But the biggest surprise of all is the tomato—new and exciting recipes featuring this favorite include a novel use for tomatoes that haven't yet reached their peak, Country Fried Tomatoes (page 78). Plum Tomato Chutney (page 77), a tempting combination of tomatoes, pine nuts, raisins and ginger, makes a delightful accompaniment for curries. There is also an updated version of the traditional stuffed tomato with a colorful filling of rice, green onion, green pepper and pimiento, all dressed with a simple vinaigrette (page 78).

Other vegetable-fruits covered are peppers of all sizes, shapes and hues, chilies and olives. Some are excellent hostess gifts—Olives Riviera (page 74) and Red Pepper Relish (page 71) in particular—but all of them are welcome additions to any cook's recipe file.

 *Avocado*

Avocado Mousse

4 servings

2 avocados
¼ cup mayonnaise
1½ teaspoons unflavored gelatin softened in 1½ teaspoons fresh lemon juice
1½ to 2 teaspoons grated onion
½ teaspoon Worcestershire sauce
½ teaspoon salt

¼ teaspoon freshly ground pepper
¼ teaspoon paprika
4 drops hot pepper sauce
2 to 3 tablespoons sour cream

Cucumber slices (garnish)

Puree avocados in processor or blender. Add remaining ingredients except sour cream and garnish. Mix well. Turn into serving bowl. Whip sour cream lightly with fork and spread quickly over mousse to prevent discoloration. Refrigerate overnight or until set.

Serve cold, garnished with cucumber slices.

Avocado Tempura with Nuts and Cheese

4 to 6 appetizer servings

1 large firm-ripe avocado, peeled, seeded and coarsely chopped
1 green onion, minced
4 generous dashes hot pepper sauce
Juice of ½ lemon
¼ teaspoon salt
⅛ teaspoon freshly ground pepper
Generous pinch of ground coriander

3 ounces salted cashews, coarsely chopped
1½ ounces Monterey Jack cheese, shredded

Peanut oil for deep frying
Tempura Batter (see following recipe)
Salt

Combine first 7 ingredients in medium bowl and mix with fork. Add nuts and cheese and toss lightly just to combine.

Heat oil to 390°F. Shape avocado mixture into balls about ½ inch in diameter. When oil is hot, dip balls into batter and deep fry no more than 5 at a time until golden, about 1 to 2 minutes, making sure oil remains at 390°F at all times. Remove with slotted spoon and drain on paper towels. Sprinkle with salt and serve immediately.

Tempura Batter

1 cup ice water
¾ cup plus 1 tablespoon sifted all purpose flour

1 egg yolk
¼ teaspoon salt
Generous pinch of baking soda

Mix all ingredients in processor or blender. Use immediately.

 Eggplant

Eggplant Cream

6 servings

1 1-pound eggplant

¼ cup minced fresh parsley
2 to 3 tablespoons fresh lemon juice
2 garlic cloves, crushed

Salt and freshly ground pepper
⅓ cup olive oil
Pita bread or Armenian cracker bread
Assorted crudités

Preheat oven to 350°F. Set unpeeled eggplant in baking dish. Bake for 30 minutes. Turn eggplant over and continue baking until completely soft, about 30 more minutes.* Peel off skin and discard.

Transfer pulp to processor or blender. Add parsley, 2 tablespoons lemon juice, garlic, salt and pepper and mix until smooth. With machine running, add olive oil in thin steady stream and mix until creamy. Taste and adjust seasoning with salt, pepper and remaining lemon juice if necessary. Serve with pita or Armenian cracker bread and assorted crudités.

*For smoky flavor, char bake eggplant over direct flame or barbecue until skin is blistered. Rub skin off instead of peeling.

Eggplant with Walnut Sauce

6 servings

1 eggplant (1½ to 2 pounds)

Salt

¾ cup chopped walnuts
1 medium garlic clove
Cayenne pepper
1½ tablespoons white wine vinegar*

3 tablespoons (about) cold water*
1 tablespoon minced fresh basil (optional)

Minced fresh parsley and pomegranate seeds (garnish)

Discard stem and hull from top of eggplant. Using long-handled fork, prick skin in several places, then insert fork through eggplant. Broil over charcoal (preferably) or gas flame, turning frequently until flesh is very soft and juicy and skin is charred (if you are using an electric oven, place eggplant on baking sheet and broil 4 inches from heat about 25 minutes, turning to char evenly).

When eggplant is cool enough to handle, squeeze gently to remove bitter juices. Peel off skin, remove overly charred spots and slit eggplant open. Scoop out seeds and discard. Chop pulp finely and season with salt.

In processor or blender chop walnuts to a paste with garlic and cayenne. Blend in vinegar and enough water to make thick sauce. Add basil and eggplant pulp and mix well. Taste and adjust seasoning. Cover and chill.

Serve sprinkled with parsley and garnished with pomegranate seeds.

*Fresh pomegranate juice can be substituted for the vinegar and water.

🥭 Eggplant

Despite its subtle flavor, its beauty of form and startling color, no vegetable evokes such extreme reactions as the eggplant—utter rejection on one side and delight, even rapture, on the other.

Eggplant. Perhaps if Americans had adopted the lilting name *aubergine* from the French, this compliant vegetable, so versatile for stuffing, frying and marinating, would attract more favorable notice. Even novice cooks in this country would look to it for daily improvisations, which is a common practice in Mediterranean and Eastern countries.

Italians have placed the eggplant on a pedestal in the kitchen, as have the Turks and Armenians, who consider it a staple, boasting of having 365 recipes, one for each day of the year. The Greeks, who gave us moussaka, have many other main dish and salad inventions as well. The Arabs rarely see the buffet table, without *baba ghanouj,* a simple puree of roasted eggplant and sesame paste. In India, where eggplant cookery is said to have originated, it is added to *kheemas* and curries for dramatic flavor and visual enhancement.

Perhaps because of the prosaic company it keeps in our gardens among the cabbages, rutabagas, beets, squash and turnips, the eggplant has been overlooked by Americans too long.

A notion still persists that an eggplant, which, like the tomato, is technically a fruit, must have the juice pressed from it before it is used. Almost all old recipes caution, "Slice, salt and press to extract the juice." Sometimes this process takes an hour or more and is, in my experience, completely unnecessary if the eggplant is firm and fresh. The purpose of salting or soaking in brine is to draw off moisture and bitterness and to prevent the flesh from absorbing too much oil during frying. Remember that the heavier the eggplant is in relation to its size, the less absorbent it will be and the lower proportion of bitter seeds it will have—thus eliminating the need to salt.

Long, narrow eggplants are usually more meaty and have fewer seeds than larger ones. The latter are often baked until soft, then the center is mashed with cooked onion, olive oil and seasonings and served as a dip known as poor man's caviar. Slices of unpeeled fried eggplant are used to line a mold filled with cooked ground lamb in moussaka. Eggplant is also good cut into little strips, dipped into a batter of beer or egg whites and deep fried. It is an essential ingredient of the famous Provence ratatouille—a stew of eggplant, onion, garlic, olive oil, tomato—served either hot or cold.

Eggplant Caviar

Great with toast, pita bread or Armenian cracker bread. Must be prepared at least 24 hours ahead so flavors mellow.

25 servings

Oil
Salt
5 medium eggplants

1¼ cups chopped fresh parsley
5 tablespoons white vinegar
2½ tablespoons fresh lemon juice
2½ tablespoons crushed fresh mint leaves

2½ teaspoons salt
1½ teaspoons granulated garlic
1¼ teaspoons freshly ground white pepper
¾ teaspoon ground cinnamon

Preheat oven to 350°F. Oil rimmed baking sheet and sprinkle with salt. Halve eggplant lengthwise and set cut side down on baking sheet. Bake until eggplant is tender, about 45 minutes. Remove from oven and let stand until cool enough to handle. Peel eggplant; finely chop pulp. Transfer to colander and let stand briefly to drain.

Thoroughly combine eggplant with remaining ingredients in large bowl. Cover and refrigerate at least 24 hours. Adjust seasoning if necessary.

Smoked Eggplant Salad

4 to 6 servings

2 medium eggplants, peeled and cut lengthwise into slices ½ inch thick
Salt

½ cup Greek olive oil

Dressing
½ cup coarsely chopped flat-leaf parsley

¼ to ⅓ cup Greek olive oil
5 green onions, thinly sliced on the diagonal
4 ripe large tomatoes, seeded and coarsely chopped
2 large garlic cloves, minced
Juice of 1½ to 2 lemons
Salt and freshly ground pepper

Layer eggplant slices in large colander and sprinkle with salt. Let drain 30 minutes. Rinse under cold water, drain well and pat dry with paper towels.

Prepare fire (coals could be either quite hot or at burning down stage to coordinate easily with other foods). Spread foil over grill and brush with about 2 tablespoons oil. Punch about 12 holes into foil.

Arrange eggplant slices on foil and cook, turning once and brushing frequently with remaining 6 tablespoons oil, until softened, about 20 minutes (eggplant should be blistered and lightly browned). Let cool.

Cut eggplant into strips about ½ inch wide and 2 to 3 inches long. Transfer to bowl. Add all ingredients for dressing and toss well. Let stand at room temperature about 2 hours before serving.

Salad can be prepared 1 day ahead and refrigerated. Serve at room temperature.

Broiled Eggplant Japanese Style (Eggplant Shigiyaki)

A delicately flavored appetizer or accompaniment to rice, meat or fish dishes.

6 to 8 servings

3 tablespoons miso* (bean paste)
3 tablespoons chicken stock
1 tablespoon mirin* (Japanese sweet wine) *or* sweet Sherry
1 teaspoon sugar

3 Japanese eggplants, unpeeled and sliced into ¼-inch rounds
¼ cup oil
Toasted sesame seed

Combine first 4 ingredients in small saucepan and bring to simmer over medium heat. Cover and keep warm.

Preheat broiler. Skewer eggplant slices sideways on wooden sticks so they lie flat. Repeat until all rounds are skewered. Brush both sides with oil and place on baking sheet. Broil 6 to 8 inches from heat source until lightly browned. Remove from broiler and brush generously from reserved sauce. Return to oven and broil about 1 more minute. Sprinkle lightly with sesame seed and serve immediately.

*Available in oriental markets.

Eggplant Custards (Papetons d'Aubergine)

Papetons d'Aubergine was created in the fourteenth century by the French Papal chef in Avignon, hence the name papeton. *A delicate creation that can be made in a large mold or in individual servings, it is excellent by itself for lunch or light supper, as well as with a roasted saddle of lamb or veal roast.*

8 servings

2 pounds small firm eggplant

3½ teaspoons salt

1 cup peanut oil
2 medium garlic cloves, crushed

6 eggs
1 cup whipping cream

Tomato Sauce (see following recipe)

Generously butter 8 small molds or a 1½- to 2-quart mold; set aside.

Peel eggplant with vegetable peeler, keeping skin as thin as possible. Blanch a few strips of skin for 1 minute in boiling water. Drain and cool under cold water. Set aside for garnish.

Slice eggplant into rounds ½ inch thick. Sprinkle with 2 teaspoons salt and spread slices on baking sheet. With point of knife, score both sides of each slice to form diamonds. Place another baking sheet on top and weight down with cans or other heavy objects. Let stand 30 minutes. (This salting and pressing removes some of the eggplant's bitter juices and prevents slices from absorbing excess oil during cooking.)

Preheat oven to 375°F. Blot eggplant with paper towels. Heat about 3 tablespoons oil in skillet, add eggplant a few slices at a time and fry on both sides until lightly browned. Transfer slices to colander to allow some of oil to drain. Repeat, adding oil as necessary. *If there are many seeds, put eggplant slices through food mill.* Puree with garlic in processor. Add eggs and blend well. Mix in whipping cream and remaining salt.

Cut blanched eggplant skin into flowers or different patterns. Decorate bottom(s) and sides of mold(s).* Carefully fill with eggplant mixture. Place piece of buttered parchment paper over top. Set mold(s) in skillet and add hot water to reach about halfway up. Bake until set, 25 to 30 minutes. Remove from water bath and let stand 10 to 15 minutes before unmolding. If decoration sticks to mold, remove carefully and rearrange on top of eggplant. Pour generous amount of tomato sauce into serving plate(s), arrange mold(s) as desired and serve immediately. Pass remaining sauce.

*Papetons can also be decorated with blanched eggplant skin after being baked.

Tomato Sauce

3 tablespoons olive oil
1 cup finely chopped onion
3 garlic cloves, crushed and chopped
2½ pounds ripe tomatoes, cut into large chunks

1½ teaspoons salt
½ teaspoon freshly ground white pepper
¼ teaspoon sugar
1 tablespoon unsalted butter

Heat oil in heavy-bottomed saucepan over medium heat. Add onion and sauté 2 minutes. Add garlic and stir briefly. Add tomatoes, cover and cook about 10 minutes. Add salt, pepper and sugar and stir well. Puree into saucepan through food mill or strainer with fine holes. Add butter bit by bit until well blended. Taste for seasonings and correct with salt and pepper if needed.

Eggplant Parmigiana alla Saltato

4 servings

1 medium eggplant, peeled and cut into ¼-inch cubes
1 teaspoon salt

¼ cup olive oil
¼ cup minced onion
2 tablespoons minced green bell pepper
2 tablespoons finely chopped fresh basil or 2 teaspoons dried, crumbled

1 garlic clove, minced
¼ teaspoon rosemary
4 medium tomatoes, cubed
½ pound shredded mozzarella cheese

Place eggplant in colander and sprinkle with salt. Let stand 30 minutes to drain. Pat dry with paper towels.

Place large skillet over high heat until very hot, about 30 seconds. Add oil, coating bottom evenly. Add onion, pepper, basil, garlic and rosemary and stir-fry 3 minutes. Add eggplant and continue to stir-fry until lightly browned, about 5 minutes. Add tomatoes and stir-fry 1 minute. Remove from heat and sprinkle with mozzarella. Turn mixture onto heated platter and serve immediately.

Oven-Fried Eggplant (Dito d'Oro)

4 to 6 servings

¾ cup seasoned breadcrumbs
¼ cup freshly grated Parmesan cheese
1 medium eggplant, peeled and sliced into 1 × 4-inch strips

½ cup oil

Freshly grated Parmesan cheese

Preheat oven to 375°F. Line baking sheet with foil. Combine breadcrumbs and Parmesan. Toss eggplant strips in oil and roll in breadcrumb mixture.

Place on baking sheet and bake until crisp and golden, about 15 to 20 minutes. Sprinkle with additional Parmesan and serve immediately.

Arabic Eggplant Eggah

6 *servings*

1 medium eggplant (about 1 pound), trimmed
2 teaspoons salt

6 tablespoons (about) olive oil

2 large red bell peppers
10 eggs
1 medium tomato, peeled, seeded and cut into ½-inch cubes
3 tablespoons coarsely chopped toasted walnuts

1½ tablespoons minced green onion
1 tablespoon minced fresh mint
Salt and freshly ground pepper

1½ teaspoons fresh lemon juice
4½ tablespoons olive oil

Mint sprigs (garnish)

Cut eggplant lengthwise into 9 to 11 slices. Arrange slices on wire rack over rimmed baking sheet. Sprinkle both sides with salt. Cover with another baking sheet and weight with heavy object. Let eggplant drain 1 hour. Rinse under cold running water; pat dry.

Heat 3 tablespoons olive oil in heavy 12-inch skillet over medium-high heat. Add eggplant in batches and cook, turning once, until tender and golden on both sides, about 3 minutes, adding more oil to skillet as necessary. Drain eggplant on paper towels.

Preheat broiler. Place red peppers on broiler pan and broil 6 inches from heat source, turning until completely blackened on all sides. Place in plastic bag and seal tightly. Let stand 10 minutes to steam. Peel peppers; discard stem and seeds. Rinse if necessary, pat dry and cut into ¼-inch julienne. Mix eggs in large bowl. Blend in red pepper, tomato, walnuts, green onion and mint. Season to taste with salt and pepper.

Measure lemon juice into cup. Slowly whisk in 1½ tablespoons olive oil. Set aside. Heat 3 tablespoons olive oil in heavy 12-inch skillet over low heat. Sprinkle cooked eggplant with salt and pepper. Arrange in skillet with slices overlapping and narrow ends pointed toward center. Pour egg mixture over. Cook until all but surface of eggah is gently set, about 15 to 20 minutes. Preheat broiler. Place eggah under broiler until top is set, 20 to 30 seconds. Brush with some of lemon juice mixture. Invert eggah onto serving platter. Brush top with remaining lemon mixture. Garnish with mint. Serve hot or warm.

Armenian Stuffed Eggplant (Karni Yarek)

4 to 6 *servings*

4 small eggplants, unpeeled

¼ cup olive oil
½ pound lean ground lamb or beef
1 medium onion, chopped
1 garlic clove, minced
¼ teaspoon allspice
¼ cup pine nuts or chopped walnuts

2 tablespoons minced fresh parsley
Salt and freshly ground pepper

½ cup drained, chopped canned tomatoes
⅓ cup breadcrumbs

8 thin slices fresh tomato (garnish)

Cut eggplant in half lengthwise and scoop out pulp. Reserve shells. Coarsely chop pulp, discarding all dark, seedy portions. Set aside.

Heat oil in large skillet over medium-high heat. Add meat, onion, garlic, allspice, nuts, parsley, salt and pepper and cook until meat is browned and onion is tender. Use slotted spoon to transfer mixture to small bowl.

Preheat oven to 350°F. In small skillet, sauté reserved eggplant pulp until lightly browned. Return meat mixture to skillet, add tomatoes and half of breadcrumbs and stir constantly until heated through. Spoon into reserved eggplant shells, sprinkle with remaining breadcrumbs and garnish with tomato. Place on baking sheet or in large shallow baking dish, cover loosely with foil and bake until fork tender, about 45 minutes. Serve immediately.

Serbian Musaka

12 servings

2 medium or 3 small eggplants
Salt

⅔ cup olive oil
Flour

5 eggs, beaten

Oil
3 large onions, diced
1 pound ground lamb
½ pound ground pork, trimmed of all fat
½ pound lean ground beef
2 garlic cloves, minced
2 eggs, lightly beaten
¼ cup breadcrumbs

Generous dash of freshly grated nutmeg
Generous dash of dried basil
Dash of cinnamon
Salt and freshly ground pepper

6 tablespoons (¾ stick) butter
6 tablespoons flour
2 cups milk
3 egg yolks, beaten
Salt and freshly ground white pepper

Sour cream

Cut unpeeled eggplant lengthwise into slices ¼ inch thick. Place in colander, sprinkle with salt and let stand for about 30 minutes to drain.

Rinse eggplant thoroughly and pat dry. Heat olive oil in large skillet until very hot. Dust eggplant slices with flour and dip in beaten egg. Brown quickly on both sides in batches. Remove with slotted spoon; drain on paper towels.

Heat small amount of oil in 12-inch skillet over medium-high heat. Add onion and sauté until translucent. Add lamb, pork, beef and garlic and continue cooking until meats are crumbly and lightly browned. Drain fat. Add lightly beaten eggs and mix well. Blend in breadcrumbs, nutmeg, basil, cinnamon and salt and pepper.

Melt butter in small saucepan over medium heat. Add flour and stir constantly until smooth. Slowly add milk and stir until thickened. Blend a little of this mixture into beaten yolks, then add to saucepan. Season to taste with salt and pepper.

Preheat oven to 375°F. Oil 9 × 13-inch baking dish. Arrange layer of eggplant in dish. Top with layer of meat mixture. Repeat, ending with layer of eggplant. Pour sauce over and bake 1 hour. Cut into squares. Serve with sour cream.

Hasamiage Eggplant

4 to 5 servings

½ cup uncooked shrimp, cleaned and deveined
Salt
Flour
1 green onion, minced
1 piece (about 1-inch cube) fresh ginger, grated
1 to 2 eggs, beaten

Oil for deep frying
4 to 5 Japanese eggplants (about 2 × 4 inches), peeled and halved lengthwise
Breadcrumbs
Soy sauce flavored with fresh ginger

Mash shrimp with back of heavy cleaver or large knife. Transfer to bowl and sprinkle lightly with salt and flour. Mix in onion and ginger with just enough beaten egg to hold mixture together.

Heat oil in deep fryer to 375°F. Scrape out small amount of pulp from eggplants to allow room for shrimp mixture. Fill with shrimp, dip in remaining egg and breadcrumbs and fry until golden brown and tender, about 3 to 4 minutes. Serve immediately with soy sauce flavored with piece of fresh ginger.

Eggplant "Crepes" Sorrento

A hearty meatless do-ahead dish that can be doubled easily or even tripled for a party.

6 to 8 servings

4 medium eggplants, cut into ¼-inch-thick slices lengthwise (about 6 to 7 slices per eggplant)
Salt

Olive oil

Mushroom-Cheese Filling
  1 tablespoon olive oil
  1 large onion, minced
  ¾ pound fresh mushrooms, sliced
  ¼ cup (about) dried mushrooms (preferably cèpes*), soaked in ½ cup warm water 30 minutes and drained well (reserve liquid)
  Salt and freshly ground pepper
  ¾ pound ricotta cheese
  ½ cup *each* freshly grated Parmesan and Romano cheeses, preferably imported (about 2½ ounces each)
  3 green onions, chopped
  1 egg
  1 tablespoon chopped fresh basil leaves or ¾ teaspoon dried, crumbled

  ½ teaspoon chopped fresh oregano or ⅛ teaspoon dried, crumbled
  ½ teaspoon minced fresh mint leaves or ⅛ teaspoon dried, crumbled

Tomato-Basil Sauce
  2 tablespoons olive oil
  1 large onion, minced
  1 large garlic clove, minced
  1½ teaspoons chopped fresh basil leaves or generous ½ teaspoon dried, crumbled
  Generous pinch of dried oregano, crumbled
  3 cups tomato puree
  1 tablespoon tomato paste
  Salt and freshly ground pepper

  6 ounces mozzarella or scamorza** cheese, shredded

Place eggplant in colander and sprinkle lightly with salt. Set aside 30 minutes to drain. Rinse under running water; pat dry with paper towels.

Preheat oven to 475°F. Brush large baking sheet with olive oil. Lightly brush 1 side of eggplant slices with oil. Arrange about ¼ of eggplant slices oiled side down on prepared baking sheet. Bake in batches until softened, about 5 minutes. (This can also be done on baking sheet lined with oiled aluminum foil; while 1 batch is baking, next can be arranged on another piece of foil.) If time allows, spread baked slices on paper towels. Top with more paper towels, then weight with heavy chopping board and let stand overnight to drain and flatten slightly.

For filling: Heat olive oil in heavy nonaluminum large skillet over very low heat. Add onion, cover and cook slowly to mellow flavor, about 30 minutes, stirring occasionally. Increase heat to high, add fresh mushrooms and sauté until lightly browned. Add dried mushrooms with liquid and cook until moisture has evaporated. Let cool. Season to taste with salt and pepper. Combine ricotta,

Parmesan, Romano, green onion, egg, basil, oregano and mint in large bowl and beat well. Blend in cooled mushroom mixture. *(Filling can be prepared 1 day ahead and refrigerated.)*

For sauce: Heat olive oil in heavy nonaluminum large skillet over very low heat. Add onion, cover and cook slowly to mellow flavor, about 30 minutes, stirring occasionally. Uncover, increase heat to medium, add garlic, basil and oregano and stir 30 seconds. Blend in tomato puree and tomato paste with salt and pepper to taste. Bring to boil. Let boil until thickened slightly, about 5 minutes. *(Sauce can be prepared 2 months ahead and frozen.)*

Grease shallow large baking dish. Spread about 1 tablespoon filling over each piece of eggplant, leaving about 1-inch border at thicker end. Starting at narrower end, roll eggplant up jelly roll style. Transfer to prepared baking dish. *(Can be prepared up to 1 day ahead to this point. Cover with plastic wrap and refrigerate.)*

Preheat oven to 375°F. Spread sauce over eggplant rolls. Sprinkle with shredded cheese. Bake until sauce is bubbling and cheese begins to color, about 45 minutes. Serve immediately.

*Available at specialty foods stores.
**A mild, chewy, slightly salty dried mozzarella traditionally made from water buffalo milk. Available at Italian markets and specialty foods stores.

Peppers and Olives

Red Pepper Relish

Makes 1½ quarts

6 cups ½-inch pieces red bell pepper
4 cups finely chopped onion
8 garlic cloves, finely minced
3 to 4 serrano or jalapeño chilies, finely minced
3 tablespoons coarse salt

1¾ to 2¼ cups sugar*
1¾ cups cider vinegar
1 tablespoon mustard seed
1 tablespoon dried oregano
1 bay leaf

Mix red pepper, onion, garlic, chilies and salt in large bowl. Let stand 3 hours. Drain thoroughly (do not rinse). Combine remaining ingredients in large saucepan and bring to boil over medium-high heat. Let boil 10 minutes. Reduce heat to medium, stir in pepper mixture and cook until peppers are translucent but still slightly crunchy, about 30 to 45 minutes.

Pour relish into 1 clean, hot pint jar to ½ inch from top. Run plastic knife or spatula between relish and jar to release any air bubbles. Clean rim and threads of jar with damp cloth. Seal with new, scalded, very hot lid. Repeat with remaining jars. Transfer to gently simmering (180°F to 190°F) water bath and process for 15 minutes. Let jars cool on rack. Test for seal. Store in cool dry place.

*Amount of sugar can be adjusted to taste: Use 2¼ cups for sweet relish; 1¾ cups for tangy. For a tarter version, use only 1 cup.

Turkish Stuffed Peppers

Makes 1 gallon

5 pounds very small green and red bell peppers (about 5 to 6 per pound)
4 quarts water
1 cup salt

4 pounds green cabbage
1½ pounds onion
1½ cups coarsely chopped celery
2 large carrots
½ cup fresh parsley
6 to 8 garlic cloves
1 quart water
2 cups white vinegar
½ cup sugar
2 tablespoons coarse salt
1 teaspoon celery seed
½ teaspoon mustard seed

4 bay leaves
6 cups water *or* 4 cups water and 2 cups olive oil
2 cups white vinegar
3 tablespoons coarse salt
1 tablespoon black peppercorns
2 teaspoons turmeric
1 teaspoon coriander seed
1 teaspoon cumin
1 teaspoon mustard seed
1 teaspoon paprika
¼ to ½ teaspoon dried red pepper flakes

Cut crown off bell peppers ¾ inch from top. Remove and discard stems, seeds and pith; reserve caps. Blend water and salt in nonmetal bowl. Add peppers and caps. Refrigerate mixture for at least 8 hours or overnight.

Drain peppers and rinse under cold water. Drain well. Finely chop cabbage, onion, celery, carrots, parsley and garlic in batches in processor using on/off turns. Transfer cabbage mixture to stockpot. Add water, vinegar, sugar, salt, celery seed and mustard seed. Place over high heat and bring to boil. Reduce heat and simmer 20 minutes.

Drain cabbage mixture well. Spoon into peppers; replace caps. Divide peppers among 4 clean, hot quart jars. Add 1 bay leaf to each jar. Combine remaining ingredients in stockpot and bring to rapid boil over high heat. Let boil 3 minutes. Ladle enough hot brine into 1 jar just to cover peppers. Run plastic knife or spatula between peppers and jar to release any air bubbles. Clean rim and threads of jar with damp cloth. Seal with new, scalded, very hot lid. Repeat with remaining jars. Transfer jars to gently simmering (180°F to 190°F) water bath and process for 30 minutes. Let jars cool on rack. Test for seal. Store in cool dry place, inverting occasionally to prevent separation if using olive oil.

Stuffed Peppers à l'Italienne

6 servings

¼ cup imported olive oil
4 tomatoes, peeled, seeded and minced
2 garlic cloves, finely minced
2 tablespoons minced fresh parsley
2 7½-ounce cans tuna (preferably packed in olive oil), drained (reserve oil)
⅔ cup homemade breadcrumbs
6 anchovy fillets, finely minced

½ cup minced green olives
2 tablespoons minced capers, rinsed
1 tablespoon minced fresh basil
Salt and freshly ground pepper

6 medium-size green bell peppers, cored and seeded
2 tablespoons olive oil (from drained tuna)

Chopped fresh parsley (garnish)

Preheat oven to 350°F. Generously oil baking dish. Heat ¼ cup olive oil in large heavy skillet over medium-high heat. Add tomatoes, garlic and parsley and cook until all tomato liquid has evaporated. Add tuna, breadcrumbs, anchovies, olives, capers, basil, salt and pepper; cook 2 minutes longer.

Carefully stuff peppers, place in prepared baking dish and drizzle with remaining olive oil. Bake 45 to 50 minutes. Cool to room temperature, then transfer to serving platter and sprinkle with chopped parsley.

For variation, add ½ cup cubed pepperoni just before stuffing peppers.

Stuffed Banana Peppers (Piperies Yemistes)

These long thin greenish-yellow peppers are perfect for stuffing, but sweet peppers or red or green bell peppers can be substituted if preferred.

10 to 12 servings

13 mild or hot banana peppers

2 tablespoons olive oil
1 small onion, minced
1 cup water
½ cup uncooked rice
1 medium tomato, peeled, seeded and chopped

2 tablespoons minced fresh parsley
½ teaspoon salt
¼ teaspoon dried dillweed

¼ cup tomato puree

Cut ½ inch off tops of peppers and set aside. Remove cores and seeds with long thin knife. Rinse peppers in cold water to remove any remaining seeds; pat dry. Heat oil in heavy large skillet over medium-high heat. Add onion and sauté 10 minutes. Stir in ½ cup water, rice, tomato, parsley, salt and dillweed. Cook until liquid evaporates, about 10 minutes. Remove from heat.

Preheat oven to 350°F. Cut 1 pepper in half lengthwise and set aside. Fill remaining peppers loosely with rice mixture; replace tops. Position 2 pepper halves against long side of rectangular baking dish. Prop stuffed peppers against pepper halves, stacking in dish as necessary. Combine remaining ½ cup water with tomato puree in small bowl and blend well. Pour over peppers. Cover and bake 45 to 50 minutes. Serve hot with sauce accumulated in dish or pass separately.

Peppers can be filled 1 day ahead and refrigerated, or frozen up to two weeks. Defrost in refrigerator before baking.

Chilies in Walnut Sauce (Chiles en Nogada)

6 servings

Chilies
6 very fresh Anaheim chilies
¼ cup oil
¼ cup vinegar
½ medium onion, diced
2 bay leaves
½ teaspoon dried oregano
½ teaspoon dried thyme
1 garlic clove, crushed

Filling
2 tablespoons oil
1 pound ground beef
1 medium onion, diced
1 garlic clove, minced

Salt and freshly ground pepper
½ cup peeled diced tomatoes
½ cup raisins, plumped in water 15 minutes, drained
½ cup slivered almonds

Sauce
1 cup walnuts
6 ounces cream cheese
¼ cup milk
3 garlic cloves or more to taste
Salt

Pomegranate seeds* (optional garnish)

For chilies: Peel chilies according to directions in boxed copy, facing page. Place in medium saucepan and cover with water. Add oil, vinegar, onion, bay leaves, oregano, thyme and garlic. Bring to rapid boil over high heat, then reduce heat and simmer 20 minutes, or until chilies feel soft when pricked with fork. Cool in liquid; drain.

For filling: Heat oil in medium skillet over medium heat. Add meat, onion and garlic and cook, stirring and separating meat with a fork, until all pink disappears. Season with salt and pepper to taste. Stir in tomatoes, raisins and almonds and cook about 10 minutes longer, stirring frequently.

Divide filling among chilies. Arrange on plate, slightly pinching chilies together with fingers to enclose filling.

For sauce: Combine all ingredients except garnish in blender or processor and mix well. Spoon over chilies.**

Garnish chilies with pomegranate seeds for traditional red, white and green colors that distinguish this dish. Serve at room temperature.

*Pomegranate seeds may be frozen. Place on baking sheet or flat dish, freeze quickly, then transfer to plastic bags.
**The sauce also makes an excellent dip for tortilla chips.

Olives Riviera

After serving, any remaining oil can be reused for brushing on lamb or poultry before grilling, drizzling on pizzas before baking, moistening toast for canapés or sautéing fresh mushrooms.

Makes 1 quart cured olives

4 cups assorted mixed cured olives, slashed on 1 side with sharp, very thin knife
Lemon peel spiral(s) from 1 large lemon (yellow part only)
8 large garlic cloves, quartered
1 medium onion, sliced
6 to 8 anchovy fillets (to taste)

1 1-inch sprig fresh rosemary or 1 teaspoon dried, crumbled
1 tablespoon Herbes de Provence or 1 teaspoon *each* dried rosemary, lavender, oregano and fennel seed, crumbled
Olive oil

Using crock or nonaluminum bowl, make about 8 even layers of ½ cup olives, piece of lemon peel, garlic clove, onion slice, anchovy fillet, rosemary and Herbes de Provence. Cover mixture with olive oil. Store in cool dark place for at least 3 days or up to 1 week.

🍎 Know Your Chilies

Chilies come in such a vast array of types that it would be impossible to list them all here. Additionally, they tend to cross-fertilize, so there can be unexpected variations within each species. To confuse matters further, the same chili sometimes goes under a different name depending on locale.

Basically, chilies are divided into the dried red type and the green variety (usually employed fresh, canned or pickled). The following glossary should help identify similar varieties, so you can choose appropriate substitutes.

Reds (Dried)

Ancho: This is the all purpose dried red chili. It is about 2 to 5 inches long, broad, full flavored and rather mild. Fresh, it's the chili *poblano.*

Mulato: Same shape as the *ancho,* but brownish black in color, a little larger and with a sweeter flavor.

Pasilla: About 7 inches long, very dark red and more pungent, though not as rich in flavor as either the *ancho* or *mulato.* Fresh, it's the chili *chilaca.*

Chipotle: Light brown, smoked, about 2¾ inches long, it is the ripened, dried *jalapeño.* It's very hot.

Greens (Fresh, Canned)

Anaheim: Long green chili, mild. Also called California green chili. When canned, labeled "green chili."

Serrano: A small, tapering all purpose mild green chili sold fresh or canned. The fresh, long chili *cayenne* can be substituted if *serrano* unavailable.

Poblano: This is dark green, can be mild or hot. Not readily available in the United States. Use canned, peeled green chilies as a substitute.

Jalapeño: This small, green hot chili is available fresh in California and the Southwest as well as canned in other parts of the country.

Güero: A very pale yellowish chili, the *güero* averages 4 to 5 inches, can vary from hot to very hot. Available canned from California.

Handling Chilies

Oils in the flesh and seeds can make eyes water and skin smart. Wearing rubber gloves is a wise precaution. Be careful not to rub face or eyes after fingers have touched the chilies, and wash hands thoroughly when finished.

Rinse chilies in cold water and remove stems. Partially split each chili and brush out the seeds with fingers. Removing the veins will lessen the pungency. A pair of small scissors simplifies the task.

Dried chilies should be torn into small pieces, covered with boiling water and soaked for 10 minutes to an hour before use; fresh ones used immediately.

Peeling fresh chilies: Pour ½ inch to 1 inch of oil in a skillet and heat. Place chilies in hot oil until they blister. Turn and allow the other side to blister. Remove from oil and wrap in a damp towel. Skins will slip off easily.

Canned chilies should be rinsed in cold water to remove the brine in which they were preserved. Be careful not to get the pickled ones (*en escabeche*) unless called for: Pickling cannot be rinsed away.

Tomatoes

Tomatoes Pesto

16 servings

2 cups tightly packed fresh basil leaves or 1 cup basil leaves and 1 cup fresh parsley
½ cup olive oil
2 tablespoons pine nuts
3 garlic cloves, chopped

½ teaspoon salt
Freshly ground pepper
½ cup freshly grated Parmesan cheese
2 pints cherry tomatoes, halved

Combine basil, oil, pine nuts, garlic, salt and pepper in processor or blender and mix until smooth. Stir in Parmesan. *(Pesto can be prepared several days ahead, covered tightly and refrigerated.)* Drain tomatoes cut side down on paper towels. Spoon small amount of pesto onto each tomato half. Chill until ready to serve.

Tomato Relish

May be served as a mild side dish for Mexican entrées such as chiles relle-nos or enchiladas. Also good with steaks or chops.

Makes about 1 quart

3 medium tomatoes, peeled and diced
1 green bell pepper, seeded and diced
1 onion, finely chopped
½ cup finely chopped celery

¼ cup vinegar
¼ cup sugar
1½ teaspoons salt
¼ teaspoon freshly ground pepper
¾ to 1 cup cold water

Combine tomatoes, pepper, onion and celery in large bowl. Mix vinegar, sugar, salt and pepper in small bowl. Add water to vinegar mixture as desired. Pour over vegetables. Cover and refrigerate at least 8 hours, preferably overnight. Drain mixture thoroughly before serving.

Chunky Tomato Sauce

Makes 2 to 2½ cups

1 tablespoon butter
1 tablespoon olive oil
1 small onion, chopped
2 garlic cloves, minced
2 2-pound 3-ounce cans peeled whole Italian plum tomatoes, drained and coarsely chopped
½ teaspoon dried basil, crumbled

½ teaspoon salt
1 bay leaf
Pinch of dried thyme, crumbled
Pinch of sugar (optional)
Freshly ground pepper
3 tablespoons chopped fresh parsley

Melt butter with olive oil in heavy large saucepan over medium heat. Add onion and cook 5 minutes. Add garlic and cook 2 minutes. Stir in all remaining ingredients except parsley. Increase heat to medium high and boil, stirring frequently, until mixture is thickened, about 10 to 20 minutes. Discard bay leaf. Taste and adjust seasoning. *(Can be prepared 3 days ahead to this point, cooled, covered and refrigerated; sauce can also be frozen. Reheat before serving.)* Just before serving, stir in parsley.

Plum Tomato Chutney

Makes about 3 cups

8 garlic cloves
½ cup finely chopped crystallized ginger
1½ cups red wine vinegar
1 35-ounce can plum tomatoes, undrained

1½ cups sugar
2 teaspoons salt
½ teaspoon dried red pepper flakes
½ cup pine nuts
½ cup golden raisins

Combine garlic, ginger and ½ cup vinegar in processor or blender and puree until smooth. Transfer to large saucepan. Add tomatoes (with liquid), remaining 1 cup vinegar, sugar, salt and red pepper flakes. Place over medium-high heat and bring to boil. Reduce heat to low and simmer until mixture coats spoon, about 2 hours. Blend in pine nuts and raisins and simmer 5 more minutes. Let cool. Transfer to jar(s) with tight-fitting lid(s). Refrigerate until ready to serve.

Marinated Tomatoes with Cilantro

4 to 6 servings

6 medium tomatoes, sliced
¼ cup chopped fresh cilantro (also known as coriander or Chinese parsley)
3 tablespoons white wine vinegar
2 tablespoons olive oil
2 tablespoons safflower oil
1 garlic clove, minced

½ teaspoon mayonnaise
¼ teaspoon brown sugar
¼ teaspoon Dijon mustard
Salt and freshly ground pepper
Hard-cooked egg wedges (garnish)

Arrange tomatoes in shallow serving bowl, quiche dish or plate and sprinkle evenly with cilantro. Combine vinegar, oils, garlic, mayonnaise, sugar and mustard in small jar and shake well. Pour evenly over tomatoes. Cover and chill well. Season with salt and pepper just before serving and garnish with eggs.

Chilled Vegetable-Stuffed Tomatoes

To keep tomatoes from falling over on the serving plate, set the sliced-off tops beneath each tomato as a base.

8 to 12 servings

Marinade
½ cup corn oil
¼ cup vinegar or fresh lemon juice
1 tablespoon water
1 garlic clove, crushed
1 large pinch of paprika
¼ teaspoon Dijon mustard
Salt and freshly ground pepper

2 cups frozen peas, cooked briefly
1 small head cauliflower, cut into florets and cooked crisp-tender
1 cup cubed carrots, cooked crisp-tender
1 bunch green onions, finely chopped
½ cup chopped fresh parsley

8 to 12 medium tomatoes

Combine all ingredients for marinade in large mixing bowl and blend well.

Add peas, cauliflower, carrots, onion and parsley and toss lightly but thoroughly. Cover and chill about 5 hours, tossing two or three times.

Cut tops off tomatoes and set aside; scoop out pulp using melon baller. Invert tomatoes on paper towels and let drain for several hours. Fill tomatoes with vegetable mixture and chill about 3 hours before serving.

Stuffed Tomatoes à la Genovese

6 to 8 servings

6 tablespoons imported olive oil
2 tablespoons red wine vinegar
1 teaspoon Dijon mustard
1 large garlic clove, crushed
Salt and freshly ground pepper

6 to 8 medium tomatoes
Salt

1 cup salted water
½ cup long-grain rice

½ to ¾ cup fresh basil leaves, tightly packed
1 to 2 tablespoons imported olive oil

2 tablespoons finely minced green onion

2 tablespoons finely minced fresh parsley
2 tablespoons finely minced green bell pepper
2 tablespoons finely minced pimiento
4 flat anchovy fillets, finely minced
Salt and freshly ground pepper

⅓ cup whipping cream
1 teaspoon Dijon mustard

Lettuce leaves

Parsley sprigs and black olives (garnish)

Combine first 4 ingredients with salt and pepper to taste in blender or processor fitted with plastic knife and mix well. Set aside.

Cut ¼-inch slice off top of each tomato. Using small sharp knife, carefully hollow out tomato, leaving shell ¼ inch thick; discard seeds. Mince pulp and reserve. Sprinkle tomatoes with salt and place them upside down on double layer of paper towels.

Bring salted water to boil in small saucepan. Add rice, reduce heat, cover and simmer 20 minutes or until tender. Transfer to colander, rinse well and drain completely. Cool 4 to 6 hours.

Combine basil leaves and olive oil and puree to fine paste. Set aside 1 tablespoon and refrigerate any remainder for use in other dishes.

Turn rice into large mixing bowl. Add green onion, parsley, green pepper, pimiento, anchovies, minced tomato pulp, 1 tablespoon of the basil paste, a small amount of vinaigrette, salt and pepper and blend thoroughly.

Whip cream in small bowl. Blend in 1 teaspoon mustard and add to rice mixture, stirring until well combined.

Place tomatoes on lettuce-lined serving platter and drizzle with remaining vinaigrette. Carefully fill with rice mixture. Garnish each with parsley sprigs and black olives. Serve slightly chilled or at room temperature.

Country Fried Tomatoes

A great dish to rescue tomatoes that are either a little too firm or too pale.

4 servings

4 firm red or green medium tomatoes, cored
½ cup whole wheat breadcrumbs
1½ to 2 teaspoons dried dillweed

¼ cup (½ stick) butter
Salt and freshly ground pepper
Cottage cheese (optional)

Slice tomatoes about ¼ inch thick. Combine breadcrumbs and dill and mix well. Coat slices on both sides with crumb-dill mixture. Melt butter in frying pan over medium heat. Add tomatoes and sauté on both sides until golden brown. Season to taste with salt and pepper. Top with cottage cheese just before serving.

6 ❧ Roots, Tubers, Onions and Mushrooms

It is interesting when comparing the varied cuisines of the world how many foods seem to be universally popular, even though they may be given entirely different treatments in different countries. That is particularly true in the case of the vegetables in this chapter.

Potatoes seem to be everyone's favorite. Undeniably versatile, they can be left whole, mashed, riced, sliced, diced, steamed, baked, boiled, fried or grilled. They are also high in vitamins and actually low in calories, despite what most people believe. This collection includes some delightful twists, such as Baked Potato Chips (page 84) as well as the completely classic fried Potatoes Dauphine (page 86). You'll also find unusual variations on the classic treatments, including Spinach-Stuffed Potatoes (page 85), Oven-Browned Potatoes with Pancetta and Rosemary (page 86) and an easy Swiss-Style Potato Cake (page 85). There are also exciting dishes for yams and sweet potatoes.

Beets and carrots add color and flavor to any menu. They are highlighted here in tempting accompaniments, from sophisticated Carrots with Pistachios and Cointreau (page 82) or Glazed Matchstick Beets (page 80) to healthful salads and country-style dishes.

Leeks have been highly prized in Europe for centuries and, along with onions and garlic, offer unlimited possibilities for the creative cook. Onions, Piedmont Style (page 97) with Italian sausage is definitely hearty fare for a cold winter night, while Poached Leeks with Tarragon-Mustard Vinaigrette (page 90) would fit nicely into a warm-weather menu as either a first course or a side dish.

We round out this collection with mushrooms. The revolution called nouvelle cuisine has introduced Americans to many imported wild mushrooms, including Italy's meaty *porcini*, *cepes* and *chanterelles* from France, and *enoki* and *shittake* from the Orient. However, the edible field mushroom is still the most frequently encountered in the American produce market. Mushroom Nachos (page 100) is a clever variation of a popular Mexican appetizer, and other good hors d'oeuvres candidates include Fresh Mushrooms with Eggplant and Tomato (page 102) or French Fried Mushrooms (page 99) with an anchovy- and caper-accented tartar sauce with chive and tarragon.

 *Beets*

Glazed Matchstick Beets

8 servings

2½ cups pear nectar
2½ to 3½ cups water
3 tablespoons butter
1½ pounds young beets, peeled and cut into matchstick julienne

2 tablespoons sugar
½ teaspoon dry mustard
½ teaspoon salt
¼ teaspoon ground ginger

Bring pear nectar and 2½ cups water to rapid boil. Meanwhile, melt butter in deep large skillet over medium-high heat. Add remaining ingredients and blend well. Pour boiling pear nectar mixture over beets and return to boil. Cook until beets are tender, stirring frequently, about 40 minutes, adding remaining water as necessary. Turn beets into dish and serve.

Beets à la Crème

6 to 8 servings

6 medium beets, greens removed

¼ cup (½ stick) unsalted butter
1½ cups whipping cream
3 tablespoons minced fresh dill

2 tablespoons finely minced fresh chives
Salt and freshly ground pepper

Bring salted water to boil in large saucepan or Dutch oven over medium heat. Add beets, cover and cook until tender, about 45 to 60 minutes. Drain; let stand until beets are cool enough to handle. Peel; cut into ¼-inch matchstick julienne.

Melt butter in heavy large skillet over medium heat. Add beets and sauté 2 minutes, shaking pan constantly to coat beets evenly. Blend in cream and continue cooking until liquid is reduced and beets are well glazed. Stir in dill and chives. Season to taste with salt and pepper and serve immediately.

 Carrots

Carrot and Yogurt Salad

4 servings

½ pound carrots, finely shredded
½ cup canned garbanzo beans
  (chick-peas), rinsed and drained
2 tablespoons oil
1½ tablespoons white wine vinegar
1½ tablespoons minced fresh dill
  or 1½ teaspoons dried

1 tablespoon sugar
  Salt and freshly ground pepper
2 to 3 tablespoons plain yogurt

Dill sprigs (garnish)

Combine all ingredients except yogurt and garnish; toss lightly. Cover and let stand several hours at room temperature or refrigerate overnight. Arrange on platter and top with yogurt and dill.
  If refrigerating overnight, bring to room temperature before serving.

Provençal Country Carrots

12 servings

1 cup water
¼ cup olive oil
¼ cup fresh lemon juice
1 tablespoon sugar
3 medium garlic cloves, slivered
  Slivered peel of 1 large lemon
2½ pounds carrots (about 12 large),
  cut diagonally into ¼-inch slices

2 tablespoons minced fresh parsley
1 tablespoon minced fresh mint
  Salt and freshly ground pepper

Chopped fresh parsley (garnish)

Combine water, olive oil, lemon juice, sugar, garlic and lemon peel in deep large skillet and bring to simmer over medium heat. Let simmer 5 to 6 minutes. Add carrots and cook, uncovered, until just crisp-tender, 3 to 4 minutes. Transfer carrots to serving bowl using slotted spoon.
  Boil liquid remaining in skillet over medium-high heat until reduced to about ⅓ cup. Pour over carrots. Add parsley and mint and toss gently. Season with salt and pepper. Cover and refrigerate up to 2 days. Let stand at room temperature for about 30 minutes before serving. Garnish with chopped parsley.

Carrots à l'Orange

6 servings

1 pound carrots, grated
2 tablespoons water
2 tablespoons (¼ stick) butter
¼ teaspoon salt

¼ teaspoon white pepper
  Pinch of brown sugar
1 tablespoon Grand Marnier

Combine carrots, water and butter in saucepan. Place over medium heat and cook until tender. Add salt, pepper and brown sugar and stir well. Just before serving, add liqueur and mix well.

Carrots with Dill and Sour Cream

6 servings

2 tablespoons (¼ stick) butter
2 pounds carrots, halved crosswise
  and cut julienne (about 4 cups)
2 teaspoons chopped fresh dill or 1
  teaspoon dried dillweed

½ cup strong chicken stock
  (preferably homemade)
1 teaspoon sugar
2 tablespoons sour cream, room
  temperature

Melt butter in heavy large saucepan over low heat. Add carrots and dill and cook 5 minutes. Stir in chicken stock and sugar and cook until carrots are crisp-tender. Transfer carrots to serving dish using slotted spoon; keep warm. Boil stock mixture over high heat until reduced to several tablespoons. Pour over carrots. Gently blend in sour cream. Serve immediately.

Carrots with Pistachios and Cointreau

6 servings

2 tablespoons (¼ stick) butter
½ cup natural pistachios, shelled
  and skinned
¼ cup Cointreau

1 pound carrots, cut diagonally into
  ¼-inch slices

3 tablespoons butter
3 tablespoons water
1 teaspoon salt

Melt 2 tablespoons butter in medium skillet over medium-high heat. Add nuts and sauté 1 minute. Stir in Cointreau. Remove from heat and set aside.

Combine carrots, 3 tablespoons butter, water and salt in large saucepan and bring to boil over medium-high heat. Reduce heat to medium-low, cover and cook until carrots are just tender, about 5 minutes. Transfer carrots to heated serving bowl using slotted spoon; keep warm. Boil cooking liquid until reduced to 2 tablespoons. Pour over carrots. Add nuts and Cointreau. Toss gently and serve.

Carrot Ring

For an attractive presentation, fill center of Carrot Ring with carefully drained French Peas (see page 45)and surround outer edge with Steamed Cauliflower (see page 29) lightly sprinkled with paprika.

6 to 8 servings

1½ cups (3 sticks) butter, room
  temperature
1 cup firmly packed brown sugar
4 eggs, separated
3 cups finely grated raw carrots
  (approximately 1 pound)
2 tablespoons cold water

2 tablespoons lemon juice
2 cups flour
1 teaspoon baking soda
2 teaspoons baking powder
1 teaspoon salt

¼ cup breadcrumbs

Preheat oven to 350°F. Cream butter and brown sugar. Add yolks and beat until thick. Add carrots, water, lemon juice, flour, baking soda, baking powder and salt. Mix thoroughly.

Beat egg whites until stiff peaks form; fold into carrot mixture. Generously oil 3-quart ring mold; dust with breadcrumbs. Turn mixture into mold. Bake 1 hour. Remove from oven and allow to cool 3 minutes before loosening edges with dull-edged knife. Turn onto heated round serving platter.

Carrot ring may be prepared the day before. Bake just before serving.

Creamy Carrot Timbales

6 servings

1 large carrot

1 pound carrots, sliced
3 tablespoons all purpose flour

4 eggs
1 cup whipping cream

¾ teaspoon salt
½ teaspoon freshly ground white pepper

Freshly grated nutmeg

Preheat oven to 375°F. Butter six ½-cup timbale molds. Line each with circle of waxed paper; butter paper. Set aside.

Cut thickest part of large carrot into six ⅛-inch slices. Scallop edges of each slice to resemble flower. Blanch slices in rapidly boiling salted water until tender. Remove with slotted spoon (retain water at boil) and drain well. Set 1 slice in bottom of each mold.

Add remaining 1 pound carrots to same water and boil until tender. Drain well. Puree in processor or blender. Transfer to medium bowl and sprinkle with flour. *(Mixture can be prepared ahead to this point and refrigerated.)*

Beat eggs with cream in another bowl until thick and lemon colored. Add salt, pepper and nutmeg and mix well. Blend into pureed carrots.

Divide mixture evenly among prepared molds. Cover each mold with circle of buttered waxed paper. Arrange timbales in shallow baking dish and add enough boiling water to come halfway up sides of molds. Bake timbales until set, about 30 minutes.

Remove molds from water. Discard waxed paper. Let stand 5 minutes. Run tip of sharp knife around edge of timbales to loosen. Invert onto platter. Discard remaining waxed paper. Serve.

❦ *Jerusalem Artichokes*

Pickled Jerusalem Artichokes

Makes 1 gallon

4 pounds Jerusalem artichokes (also known as sunchokes), scrubbed thoroughly, peeled (if desired) and quartered
16 garlic cloves
16 dried red chilies

16 black peppercorns
1 quart cider vinegar
1 quart water
¼ cup sugar
¼ cup coarse salt

Pack artichokes tightly into 8 clean, hot pint jars to ½ inch from top. Add 2 garlic cloves, 2 chilies and 2 peppercorns to each. Combine remaining ingredients in stockpot and bring to rapid boil. Pour enough hot brine into 1 jar just to cover artichokes. Run plastic knife or spatula between artichokes and jar to release any air bubbles. Clean rim and threads of jar with damp cloth. Seal with new, scalded, very hot lid. Repeat with remaining jars.

Transfer to gently simmering (180°F to 190°F) water bath and process for 25 minutes. Let cool on rack. Test for seal. Store in cool dry place.

 *Potatoes*

Baked Potato Chips

6 servings

3½ pounds red or white boiling potatoes, cut crosswise into ⅛-inch-thick slices

6 tablespoons (¾ stick) butter, melted
Salt and freshly ground pepper

Position racks in upper and lower third of oven and preheat to 500°F. Lightly grease 2 baking sheets. Arrange potato slices in single layer on prepared baking sheets. Brush generously with butter. Bake 7 minutes. Switch pan positions and continue baking until potatoes are crisp and browned around edges, about 7 to 9 minutes. Transfer to heated platter. Sprinkle with salt and pepper to taste and serve immediately.

Potatoes in Paprika Sauce

4 servings

Paprika Sauce
1 tablespoon light vegetable oil (preferably cold-pressed safflower)
1 tablespoon Hungarian sweet paprika
1 tablespoon tomato paste
1 teaspoon potato flour or cornstarch
1 cup rich chicken stock or vegetable stock
½ teaspoon finely chopped garlic

Herb or vegetable salt (optional)
Freshly ground white pepper
2 medium or large tomatoes, peeled, seeded and chopped (about 1 to 1½ cups)

4 large baking potatoes (about ½ pound each), scrubbed and dried
1 fresh tarragon sprig, chopped, or ¼ teaspoon dried, crumbled

Combine oil and paprika in large saucepan and cook over low heat until warmed through. Remove from heat. Add tomato paste and flour and blend well. Stir in stock and garlic. Season with herb salt and ground white pepper to taste. Stir in chopped tomato.

Peel potatoes and cut into round slices ¼ inch thick. Arrange slices in sauce and sprinkle with tarragon. Place over medium heat and bring to boil. Reduce heat to low and cook until potatoes are tender, about 25 to 30 minutes.

Spinach-Stuffed Potatoes

4 servings

4 large baking potatoes (about ½ pound each), scrubbed and dried

1 pound fresh spinach (about 2 bunches), stemmed and rinsed (do not dry)

2 tablespoons light vegetable oil (preferably cold-pressed safflower) or unsalted butter

1 tablespoon whole wheat pastry flour

¾ cup (or more) nonfat milk or reconstituted nonfat dry milk

3 tablespoons freshly grated Parmesan cheese

2 tablespoons freshly grated Swiss cheese

1 tablespoon whipping cream or sour cream

½ teaspoon dry mustard

Ground red pepper
Herb or vegetable salt (optional)

1 to 2 tablespoons nonfat milk or reconstituted nonfat dry milk (optional)

8 watercress sprigs (garnish)

Position rack in top third of oven and preheat to 425°F. Pierce potato skins. Bake potatoes until tender, about 1 hour. Cut thin slice off top of each potato. Carefully scoop potato pulp from shells, leaving thin layer of pulp around sides. Set shells and pulp aside.

Cook spinach, covered, in heavy medium saucepan over medium-high heat until spinach is wilted, turning leaves occasionally, about 3 to 4 minutes. Transfer to colander and drain, pressing with back of saucer to extract as much liquid as possible. Chop spinach coarsely and set aside on paper towels.

Combine 1 tablespoon oil and flour in small saucepan and cook over low heat 3 minutes, stirring constantly. Remove from heat and add ¾ cup milk. Return to low heat and bring to boil. Add 2 tablespoons Parmesan cheese, Swiss cheese, whipping cream and mustard. Simmer gently for about 4 minutes, stirring occasionally. Divide sauce in half. Stir spinach into one half.

Preheat broiler. Transfer potato pulp to large bowl of electric mixer and beat until smooth. Add remaining 1 tablespoon oil and season with ground red pepper and herb salt to taste. If puree is too stiff to pipe through pastry bag, add 1 to 2 tablespoons milk. Divide spinach mixture evenly among potato shells. Spoon reserved sauce over spinach. Transfer potato puree to pastry bag fitted with large star tip and pipe rosettes or ribbons atop sauce (or spoon puree over). Sprinkle remaining 1 tablespoon Parmesan over potatoes. Broil until tops are brown. Garnish each potato with watercress sprigs.

Swiss-Style Potato Cake

4 to 6 servings

1 egg, beaten

2 tablespoons grated Swiss cheese

¼ teaspoon freshly grated nutmeg
Salt and freshly ground pepper

1 pound baking potatoes, peeled

1 medium onion

2 tablespoons (¼ stick) butter

Sour cream and crisply cooked bacon (garnish)

Beat egg with cheese, nutmeg, salt and pepper in large mixing bowl. Grate potatoes and onion into egg mixture and blend well. Melt butter in heavy 9-inch skillet over medium-high heat. Add potato batter, spreading evenly to edges. Cook 3 minutes. Reduce heat to medium low and continue cooking until potatoes are tender and golden, about 10 to 12 more minutes. Place plate over pan and invert cake onto plate. Slide cake back into skillet. Increase heat to medium high and cook 3 minutes. Reduce heat to medium low and cook until underside is golden, about 10 more minutes. Slide cake out into platter. Cut into wedges and serve. Pass sour cream and bacon separately.

Potatoes Dauphine

You can make these airy potato puffs ahead of time and freeze them for reheating in the oven just before serving.

4 servings

1 medium boiling potato, peeled and quartered
1 egg yolk
1 tablespoon butter
½ teaspoon salt
3 tablespoons butter

Pinch of salt
½ cup water
½ cup all purpose flour
2 eggs

Oil for deep frying

Place potato in saucepan with water to cover. Bring to boil and cook over medium heat until tender. Drain. Add egg yolk, 1 tablespoon butter and ½ teaspoon salt and whip until fluffy.

Melt 3 tablespoons butter with salt in small saucepan. Add water and bring to boil. As soon as butter has melted, remove pan from heat and beat in flour all at once until smoothly blended. Return to heat and beat constantly until mixture leaves sides of pan and forms a mass, about 1 to 2 minutes. Remove from heat and beat in eggs 1 at a time until dough is smooth and well blended. Combine flour mixture with potatoes and beat well.

Heat oil for deep frying to 375°F. Drop mixture into oil by teaspoonfuls and cook until puffed and golden brown. Drain briefly on paper towels. Serve immediately, or freeze on baking sheet until firm, then pack into plastic bags or airtight containers. To reheat, bake unthawed puffs at 400°F 10 to 15 minutes.

Oven-Browned Potatoes with Pancetta and Rosemary

8 to 10 servings

6 pounds new potatoes, peeled
½ cup (1 stick) unsalted butter, room temperature
6 ounces thinly sliced pancetta (Italian bacon)* coarsely chopped, or 6 ounces bacon, blanched and chopped
½ cup light-bodied olive oil

2 tablespoons crumbled dried rosemary or 8 sprigs fresh
1 teaspoon salt
⅛ teaspoon freshly ground pepper

Fresh parsley or rosemary sprigs (garnish)

Place potatoes in deep large pot and cover with cold water. Bring to boil over high heat and cook until potatoes are still a bit firm when pierced with knife, about 15 to 20 minutes for medium potatoes; *do not overcook.*

Drain potatoes and let cool several minutes. Preheat oven to 450°F. Using all of butter, coat bottom and sides of shallow large baking pan (such as broiler pan). Cut potatoes into large chunks and add to pan. Sprinkle with remaining ingredients except garnish. *(Potatoes can be prepared 1 day ahead up to this point. Bring to room temperature before recrisping at 400°F.)*

Roast, turning often, until all butter and oil are absorbed and potatoes are very crisp, about 1 to 1¼ hours.

To serve, turn into shallow serving bowl and garnish with parsley or rosemary.

*Available at Italian markets.

🍂 Yams and Sweet Potatoes

Scalloped Yams with Chestnuts and Lime

10 servings

2¾ to 3 pounds long slender yams (5 or 6)

⅔ cup light brown sugar
6 tablespoons (¾ stick) unsalted butter
⅓ cup fresh lime juice
¼ teaspoon salt

3 tablespoons dark rum
½ cup chestnuts in heavy syrup (about 8), drained and halved or quartered (depending on size)
2 tablespoons freshly grated lime peel

Combine yams in large saucepan with just enough water to cover. Partially cover pan, place over medium-high heat and cook until yams are barely tender when pierced with knife, about 20 to 25 minutes. Drain well; let cool. Trim ends at point where yams are 1½ inches in diameter. Peel yams and cut crosswise into ½-inch slices.

Preheat oven to 400°F. Generously butter shallow 9 × 13-inch baking or gratin dish. Arrange yams in dish in rows, overlapping slightly. *(Can be made 1 day ahead. Bring to room temperature before using.)*

Combine sugar, butter, lime juice and salt in medium saucepan over low heat and stir until butter is melted. Increase heat to medium and bring to simmer. Let simmer 1 minute. Remove from heat and stir in rum. Arrange chestnuts evenly over yams. Pour butter mixture over top. Bake 15 minutes, basting twice. Sprinkle lime peel over top and continue baking until yams are tender, about 10 minutes.

Preheat broiler. Broil until chestnuts are toasted and tops of yams are browned, 1 to 2 minutes. Serve hot.

Spiced Yams

An American favorite that always appears on holiday tables. This recipe minus the salt and pepper would make a marvelous tart filling.

8 to 10 servings

4 pounds yams*
¾ cup (1½ sticks) unsalted butter, room temperature
½ teaspoon allspice
½ teaspoon cinnamon
¼ teaspoon nutmeg

¼ teaspoon ground ginger
Pinch of cloves
Salt and freshly ground pepper

1 tablespoon minced fresh parsley (garnish)

Preheat oven to 400°F. Generously grease 8- to 9-cup soufflé dish. Make 2-inch slit in center of each yam and bake until soft, about 1¼ hours. Remove from oven, reduce oven temperature to 350°F and let yams stand until cool enough to handle, about 20 minutes. Halve lengthwise and scoop pulp into large mixing bowl. Discard skins.

Add all remaining ingredients except parsley and beat well. Taste and adjust seasoning. Turn yams into soufflé dish and dot with additional butter. *(Can be prepared 4 days ahead to this point. Cover and refrigerate, then bring to room temperature before baking.)*

Bake uncovered until top is lightly browned, about 1 hour. Sprinkle with minced parsley before serving.

*Butternut or acorn squash may be substituted for yams. Halve lengthwise, scoop out seeds and place flesh down on greased baking sheet. Bake in 400°F oven until squash is easily pierced with knife, about 1 hour. Scoop out pulp and beat with 6 tablespoons (¾ stick) unsalted butter and spices.

Sweet Potato Cups

12 servings

¼ cup vinegar
6 large oranges, halved and hollowed out (reserve pulp for another use)

1 29-ounce can sweet potatoes
½ cup (1 stick) butter, room temperature
1 8¼-ounce can crushed pineapple packed in own juice, undrained

¼ teaspoon cinnamon
¼ teaspoon freshly grated nutmeg
Salt and freshly ground pepper

Chopped walnuts (garnish)

Pour water into large skillet to depth of about 2 inches. Stir in vinegar. Bring to boil over medium-high heat. Add orange halves. Cover and steam 5 minutes. Drain thoroughly on paper towels.

Preheat oven to 350°F. Butter 9 × 13-inch glass baking dish. Combine sweet potatoes, butter, pineapple, cinnamon and nutmeg in large bowl and mix thoroughly. Season with salt and pepper. Fill orange cups with mixture. Sprinkle with walnuts. Arrange oranges in dish. Bake until heated through, about 20 minutes.

Sweet Potato Bouchons

2 servings

1 small white potato, peeled
1 small sweet potato, peeled
2 tablespoons (¼ stick) butter
1 egg yolk
Freshly grated nutmeg
Salt and freshly ground pepper

Flour
1 egg, lightly beaten
Breadcrumbs
Oil for deep frying

Butter shallow 1-quart dish. Boil potatoes in enough salted water to cover until tender, about 20 minutes. Drain well. Transfer to bowl. Add butter, yolk, nutmeg, salt and pepper and mash until smooth. Spoon into dish, spreading to thickness of about 1 inch. Refrigerate until ready to use.

Shape tablespoons of mixture into small 1 × 2-inch cylinders. Dust with flour. Dip each into egg and then roll in breadcrumbs. Heat oil in heavy skillet over high heat to 375°F. Add bouchons to skillet in batches and cook until golden, about 2 to 3 minutes. Remove with slotted spoon and drain on paper towels. Transfer to dish and serve immediately.

Irwin Horowitz

From left: Spiced Yams, Broccoli and Cauliflower with Lemon Garlic, Oven-Browned Potatoes with Pancetta and Rosemary, Green Beans with Tomato-Mushroom Sauce, Sweet- Sour Onions

Eggplant "Crepes" Sorrento

Rainbow of Four Vegetable Purees

Brian Leatart

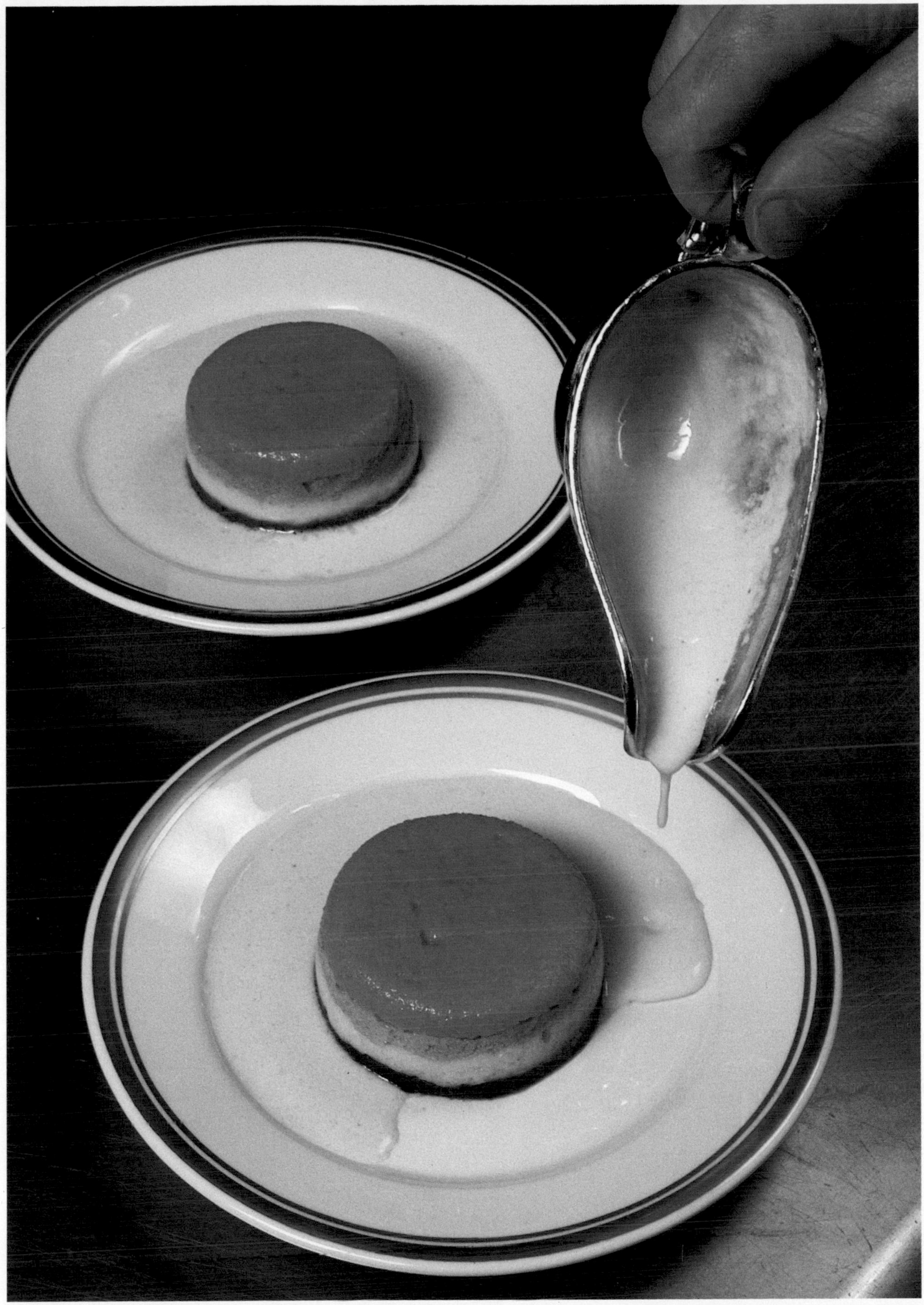

Clockwise from right:
Niçois Tart of Chard and Cheese,
Olives Riviera, Provençal Country Carrots,
Onions Monégasque

Brian Leatart

Eggplant Custard

Clockwise from right: Smoked Eggplant Salad;
Carrots with Pistachios and Cointreau;
Spinach, Catalonian Style; Spinach Chausson

Dan Wolfe

Recipes include: Curry Pickles,
Pickled Jerusalem Artichokes,
Italian Pickled Vegetables,
Turkish Stuffed Peppers, Calabrese
Cauliflower, Pickled Garlic,
Pickled Shallots, Red Pepper Relish

Brian Leatart

 *Turnips*

Spicy Creamed Turnips

8 servings

1½ to 2 pounds turnips, peeled and cut into ¼-inch cubes
½ medium onion, cut into ¼-inch cubes
3 cups water

½ cup (1 stick) butter
½ cup all purpose flour
2 cups milk

2 tablespoons white wine
1 tablespoon Dijon mustard
½ teaspoon Worcestershire sauce
½ teaspoon salt
⅛ teaspoon hot pepper sauce
¾ to 1 cup shredded sharp cheddar cheese (optional)

Combine turnip and onion in large saucepan. Add water and bring to boil over high heat. Reduce heat to medium low and simmer until vegetables are tender, about 10 minutes. Drain well, reserving 1 cup liquid.

Melt butter in large saucepan over low heat. Add flour and cook, stirring constantly, 3 to 4 minutes (do not brown). Add reserved cooking liquid, milk and wine. Increase heat to medium high, bring mixture to boil and simmer, stirring, 3 to 4 minutes. Stir in mustard, Worcestershire, salt, pepper sauce and vegetables. Serve immediately, or transfer to 9-inch square baking dish, sprinkle with cheese and bake in 350°F oven until cheese is melted, about 15 minutes.

Can be prepared ahead without cheese, transferred to 9-inch square baking dish, covered and refrigerated 1 to 2 days. Bake in 350°F oven 45 minutes. If desired, stir after 45 minutes, sprinkle with cheese and return baking dish to oven for another 15 minutes.

Turnip Fluff

4 to 6 servings

2 pounds turnips, peeled, cooked, drained and mashed
¼ cup half and half
1 egg, beaten

2 tablespoons brown sugar
2 tablespoons (¼ stick) butter
2 tablespoons uncooked farina
Salt and freshly ground pepper

Preheat oven to 350°F. Butter small baking dish (about 1 quart). Combine all ingredients in medium bowl and mix thoroughly. Spoon lightly into dish. Bake until set and top is golden, about 40 minutes.

 *Leeks*

Marinated Leeks (Poireaux Cajun)

2 servings

4 small leeks (or tender part of large leeks), thoroughly washed and drained
1 cup dry white wine

1 tablespoon tarragon vinegar
½ to 1 teaspoon Dijon mustard
½ teaspoon paprika

¼ teaspoon salt
⅛ teaspoon hot pepper sauce
3 to 4 tablespoons olive oil

Lemon wedges and carrot curls (garnish)

Combine leeks and wine in small skillet with enough water to cover. Bring to boil over medium-high heat, then reduce heat, cover partially and simmer until tender, about 15 to 20 minutes. Drain well. Transfer to serving plate.

Mix vinegar, mustard, paprika, salt and hot pepper sauce in small bowl. Add olive oil and whisk until well blended. Pour over leeks. Let stand at room temperature, turning occasionally, until leeks are cool. Cover and refrigerate until ready to serve. Garnish with lemon wedges and carrot curls.

Poached Leeks with Tarragon-Mustard Vinaigrette

A splendid accompaniment to seafood, poultry or pork.

4 servings

2 cups dry vermouth or dry white wine
3 whole cloves
10 small leeks (about 3½ pounds), split to 1 inch above root end, washed and trimmed to 6 inches above white portion

Tarragon-Mustard Vinaigrette
2 heaping teaspoons Tarragon Mustard (see following recipe)
2 teaspoons salt

½ teaspoon freshly ground pepper
¼ teaspoon sugar
¼ cup tarragon vinegar
1 cup light olive oil
2 tablespoons snipped fresh tarragon leaves

Combine vermouth and cloves in medium saucepan and bring to boil over medium-high heat. Reduce heat to low, add leeks and poach until tender, about 5 to 8 minutes. Drain well. Transfer to bowl, cover and refrigerate.

For vinaigrette: Combine mustard, salt, pepper and sugar in processor or blender and mix well. Add vinegar and mix several seconds. With machine running, add olive oil through feed tube in slow steady stream and blend until mixture thickens. Add tarragon and mix 30 seconds. Transfer to jar with tight-fitting lid and refrigerate. *(Can be prepared up to 1 week ahead.)*

To serve, arrange leeks on platter and nap with some of vinaigrette. Accompany with remaining vinaigrette.

Tarragon Mustard

A delicate creamy mustard good with cold shellfish or steamed vegetables.

Makes about 1 quart

2 cups dry mustard	1 teaspoon salt
1 cup sugar	½ cup olive oil
¾ cup tarragon vinegar	
½ cup snipped fresh tarragon or 2 tablespoons dried, crumbled	

Combine all ingredients except olive oil in processor or blender and mix until smooth and creamy. With machine running, add olive oil through feed tube in slow steady stream and blend until mixture is consistency of mayonnaise, stopping frequently to scrape down bowl. Pour into jar with tight-fitting lid and store in cool, dark place.

Leek Casserole

4 servings

¼ cup olive oil	2 tomatoes, peeled and coarsely chopped
2 large onions, coarsely chopped	1 teaspoon garlic salt
2 pounds leeks (white part only), well washed and cut into 2-inch lengths	1 teaspoon freshly ground white pepper
3 medium carrots, sliced	

Heat oil in large saucepan over medium heat. Add onions and sauté until edges are golden brown. Add leeks, carrots, tomatoes, garlic salt and pepper. Barely cover vegetables with boiling water. Simmer for 1 hour. Remove vegetables and set aside. Continue simmering liquid until reduced to ½ cup. Add vegetables and cook until heated through. Serve immediately.

 Shallots and Garlic

Pickled Shallots

Makes 1 quart

2 pounds shallots (do not peel)	2 cups water
4 fresh tarragon sprigs	¼ cup coarse salt
16 black peppercorns	3 tablespoons sugar
2 cups cider vinegar	

Bring large amount of water to rapid boil. Add shallots and blanch for 1 minute (or slightly longer if shallots are very large). Drain and rinse under cold water. Drain well. Using sharp knife, cut off roots and slip skins off shallots. Pack shallots into 4 clean, hot half-pint jars to ½ inch from top. Add 1 tarragon sprig and 4 peppercorns to each jar and set aside.

Combine all remaining ingredients in large saucepan and bring to simmer over medium-high heat. Let simmer 2 minutes. Ladle enough hot brine into 1 jar just to cover shallots. Run plastic knife or spatula between shallots and jar to release any air bubbles. Clean rim and threads of jar with damp cloth. Seal with new, scalded, very hot lid. Repeat with remaining jars. Transfer jars to gently simmering (180°F to 190°F) water bath and process for 10 minutes. Let cool on rack. Test for seal. Store pickled shallots in cool dry place.

Pickled Garlic

Much milder than you might expect. In Morocco, pickled garlic is served in small bowls along with olives.

Makes about 3½ pints

2 pounds large garlic heads, separated into cloves (do not peel)
⅓ pound fresh ginger, peeled and thinly sliced
1 cup coarse salt

7 dried red chilies
2 cups white wine vinegar
1 cup dry white wine
2½ tablespoons mustard seed

Combine garlic in large saucepan with enough water to cover. Place over medium-high heat and bring to boil. Let boil 2 minutes. Drain thoroughly. When cool enough to handle, peel each clove without crushing. Transfer to nonmetallic bowl. Add ginger and salt with enough water to cover. Refrigerate mixture for 2 days.

Drain garlic mixture and rinse thoroughly in cold water. Drain again. Pack ginger and garlic evenly into 7 clean, hot half-pint jars to ½ inch from top. Add 1 chili to each jar. Combine vinegar, wine and mustard seed in medium saucepan and bring to rapid boil over high heat. Ladle enough hot brine into 1 jar just to cover garlic mixture. Run plastic knife or spatula between mixture and jar to release any air bubbles. Clean rim and threads of jar with damp cloth. Seal with new, scalded, very hot lid. Repeat with remaining jars. Transfer jars to gently simmering (180°F to 190°F) water bath and process for 10 minutes. Let cool on rack. Test for seal. Store in cool dry place.

Small White Onions

Braised Onions

10 servings

6 tablespoons (¾ stick) unsalted butter
3 pounds small white boiling onions (about 1½ inches in diameter), blanched and peeled (see footnote to following recipe)

1 cup rich chicken stock
⅓ cup cider vinegar
2½ tablespoons sugar

Melt butter in large skillet over medium-low heat. Add onions (in 1 layer if possible) and cook until browned on all sides, 8 to 10 minutes, stirring frequently. Add stock. Cover and cook until barely tender, 18 to 20 minutes.

Pour in vinegar, sprinkle sugar over top and blend gently. Cover and cook until onions are tender when pierced with sharp knife, about 10 minutes. Uncover, increase heat to medium high and cook until liquid is syrupy, 3 to 5 minutes. Serve hot.

Onions can be prepared up to 10 hours ahead. Rewarm briefly over low heat before serving.

Sweet-Sour Onions

A new version of an old Italian recipe that is thought to date back to the Renaissance, when a cinnamon stick was traditionally added to the pot.

8 to 10 servings

5 tablespoons oil
2 pounds tiny white boiling onions, blanched and peeled*
6 tablespoons firmly packed dark brown sugar

½ cup white wine vinegar
½ cup dry white wine
1 cinnamon stick (optional)
   Salt and freshly ground pepper

Heat oil in medium saucepan over medium-high heat. Add onions and cook, stirring frequently, until they begin to take on color. Add remaining ingredients and blend well. Reduce heat to medium, cover and cook, shaking pan occasionally, until onions are tender, about 15 minutes.

Remove lid, increase heat and reduce liquid to glaze, shaking pan constantly. Transfer onions to bowl. Serve at room temperature.

Can be prepared 3 days ahead. Cover and store in refrigerator.

*To peel onions easily, drop into 3 quarts boiling water and boil 1 minute. Drain in colander. Run under cold water until onions are cool enough to handle; drain again. Cut off root and stem ends. Make shallow slit down one side and slip off skin. Cut small cross in root end to prevent bursting while cooking.

Onions Monégasque

12 servings

¼ cup olive oil
3 pounds pearl onions, peeled (see footnote to recipe above)
3 tablespoons sugar
½ cup white wine vinegar
4 firm ripe tomatoes, peeled, seeded and diced
3 garlic cloves, halved

2 bay leaves
1 teaspoon black peppercorns
1 teaspoon coriander seed
1 cup dry vermouth
   Salt
½ cup fresh parsley leaves, minced

   Chopped fresh parsley (garnish)

Heat olive oil in deep large skillet or saucepan over medium heat. Add onions and sprinkle with sugar. Cook until onions begin to color, about 4 minutes, stirring occasionally. Blend in vinegar. Increase heat to high and cook until liquid is syrupy, about 3 minutes. Stir in tomatoes, garlic, bay leaves, peppercorns and coriander seed. Add vermouth and cook until onions are tender and liquid is thickened and glossy, about 30 minutes. Add salt to taste. Stir in minced parsley. Transfer mixture to crock or glass bowl. Store in cool dark place for up to 3 days. Sprinkle onions with chopped fresh parsley and serve at room temperature.

Fried Marinated Onions à la Façon de Déjà-Vu

4 to 6 servings

1 pound pearl onions, blanched and peeled (see footnote to recipe, page 93)
2 cups white vinegar
1 cup water
2 bay leaves
2 teaspoons dill seed
2 teaspoons sugar

Oil for deep frying
½ cup all purpose flour
½ cup toasted whole wheat breadcrumbs
2 to 3 egg yolks, beaten

Combine onions, vinegar, water, bay leaves, dill seed and sugar in medium saucepan and cook over medium-high heat until onions are tender, about 5 to 10 minutes. Let cool. Cover tightly and refrigerate 48 hours.

Remove onions from marinade and drain on paper towels. Pour oil into large skillet to depth of 1 inch. Place over medium-high heat. Meanwhile, combine flour and crumbs in flat dish. Dip onions into egg, then roll in flour mixture, covering completely. When oil is hot, add onions to skillet and fry until brown and crisp. Drain on paper towels. Serve immediately.

 *Onions*

Onions Stuffed with Carrot and Spinach

6 servings

3 Spanish onions (each 3½ to 4 inches in diameter), peeled
  Pinch of herb or vegetable salt

3 medium carrots, thinly sliced
  Pinch of salt
1 pound fresh spinach, well washed and trimmed
½ teaspoon herb or vegetable salt

3 tablespoons olive oil (preferably cold-pressed)

1 teaspoon minced fresh garlic
½ cup golden or dark raisins, plumped in white wine or water and drained
¼ cup pine nuts
¾ cup sour cream

3 tablespoons freshly grated Parmesan cheese
1½ tablespoons dry whole wheat breadcrumbs

Combine onions and herb or vegetable salt in large saucepan with enough water to cover. Bring to boil over medium-low heat and let boil until onions are just softened, about 2 minutes. Drain well; pat dry with paper towels. Cut in half crosswise. Using tip of small spoon, carefully remove centers, leaving 3 outermost layers for shell. Arrange shells upright in baking dish. Finely chop centers and set aside for later use.

Place carrots and pinch of salt in small saucepan and add enough water just to cover. Bring to boil over medium-low heat; drain quickly and set aside. Place spinach in large saucepan and sprinkle with ½ teaspoon salt. Sprinkle lightly with water. Cover and cook over high heat, turning spinach frequently, until wilted, about 5 minutes. Transfer to colander and drain well, pressing with back of spoon or squeezing dry to remove as much excess moisture as possible. Cut spinach into coarse shreds.

Heat oil in large skillet over medium heat. Add chopped onion and garlic and sauté until onion is soft but not brown. Add carrots, raisins and pine nuts and continue cooking until carrots are almost tender. Increase heat to high, add spinach and cook 2 minutes, stirring constantly. Remove from heat and let cool slightly. Stir in sour cream. Taste and adjust seasoning.

Preheat broiler. Divide mixture among onions. Combine cheese and bread-crumbs and sprinkle over tops. Broil until tops are lightly golden, about 3 minutes, watching carefully to prevent burning. Serve immediately.

Onions can be filled several hours ahead and refrigerated. Warm in 325°F oven and then broil until tops are lightly browned.

Onion Confit

Makes 2½ to 3 cups

½ cup dried currants
½ cup crème de cassis

½ cup (1 stick) unsalted butter
1½ pounds medium onions (about 5), thinly sliced
⅓ to ½ cup sugar

1½ teaspoons freshly ground pepper
1 teaspoon salt

1 cup dry red wine
¼ cup vinegar (preferably red wine vinegar)

Combine currants and crème de cassis in small bowl and set aside to marinate.

Melt butter in heavy large skillet over medium heat. Stir in onion. Add sugar, pepper and salt. Cover, reduce heat to low and cook until very soft, about 30 minutes, stirring occasionally.

Pour wine and vinegar into skillet. Increase heat to medium high and cook uncovered until thickened, about 10 minutes, stirring occasionally. Drain currants; blend into onion mixture. Continue cooking until mixture is consistency of marmalade, about 10 more minutes. Serve at room temperature.

Can be prepared 3 days ahead, covered and refrigerated. Bring confit to room temperature before serving.

Onion Casserole Vinaigrette

Good choices for this dish are Walla Walla Sweets or Maui onions. You can use any onion available, but for those with strong aroma or flavor, soak chunks in milk for two hours before using.

8 servings

¼ cup (½ stick) unsalted butter
7 to 8 large onions, cut into large chunks (7 to 8 cups)

½ cup uncooked rice
5 cups boiling salted water

1 cup grated Swiss or Jarlsberg cheese

⅔ cup half and half
Salt
Vinaigrette (see following recipe) (optional)

Melt butter in large skillet over medium heat. Add onion and sauté until transparent. Remove from heat.

Preheat oven to 325°F. Cook rice in boiling salted water 5 minutes; drain well. Blend into onions along with cheese and half and half. Taste and season with salt. Turn into shallow 2-quart dish and bake 1 hour. Serve hot or chilled. Accompany with Vinaigrette if serving chilled.

🌰 *Onions*

We seldom consider singling out the onion for distinction; yet we would never want to cook without this savory gift from the lily family and its cousins—garlic, shallots, green onions, chives and leeks. All relatives of the stately amaryllis, these six distinctive herb-vegetables (herbs because of their non-woody stems) are indispensable and see more action in the kitchen than most other vegetables.

In its pristine state, each version of the edible lily has its own individual brusque—even harsh—flavor, but cooked in butter or oil or braised in a flavorful liquid, each is transformed and ready to meet the most demanding challenge. (Try any one of them when rejuvenating leftovers.)

The onion group represents one of the oldest vegetables known to man. Its bulb shape and potency have endowed it with great significance. Pliny and Herodotus refer to garlic as energy food. The slaves who built the pyramids for the Egyptian pharaohs are said to have subsisted mainly on a diet of garlic and onions. The onion was a sacred symbol for the Egyptians, who saw in its unique layer-upon-layer structure a symbol of eternity; in fact, they went so far as to take their sacred oaths with the right hand resting on an onion. And centuries of folklore have attributed curative powers to onions, garlic and leeks: They are credited with exorcising everything from vampires to the common cold.

Dozens of age-old methods have been devised for preventing weeping while chopping onions: Peeling the onions near or under cold running water; retaining the stem end intact until the last chop; closing your mouth and breathing through your nose; holding a crust of bread or celery between your teeth; and lighting a candle and keeping it close by. However, not even today's processor is guaranteed to completely solve the problem.

The edible lilies can be divided into two categories—dried and green. Whatever the dried onion, whether globe, Bermuda, Spanish, white, red-purple, shallot or garlic, it should be firm when brought home from the market. Outer skins should be dry, unspotted and clean. Avoid buying if sprouts have appeared or if necks are soft or wet. Always store in a cool, airy, dry place. Scallions, chives and leeks should have fresh green leaves and very white firm bulbs. Store in refrigerator to preserve freshness.

Yellow globe: Multipurpose and the most common. They tend to be sharper than other varieties.

Vinaigrette

6 tablespoons oil
2 tablespoons white wine vinegar
2 tablespoons finely chopped dried herbs, crumbled (such as a combination of parsley, tarragon, chives and chervil)

Salt and freshly ground pepper

Combine all ingredients in bowl or jar with tight-fitting lid and blend well.

Large golden Spanish and Bermuda: Known for their mild flavor. Delicious raw. Their sweetness makes them a good bet for onion soup.

Small white onions: Contain more water and less sugar and are commonly used for pickling, stews, or as a sauced vegetable.

Red-purple: Best eaten raw, because in the cooking their mild flavor disappears, and the onion itself tends to disintegrate. These onions are beautiful as well as delicious in salads, in the pickling of herring or marinated with cucumber slices.

Shallots: The aristocrats of the onion family. These small, brown-skinned clustered bulbs have a subtle flavor, a cross between onion and garlic. Lightly sautéed in butter, shallots provide a wonderful dimension to many dishes—bulgur wheat and rice pilafs, fish, meat and poultry dishes, stuffings and many classic sauces.

Garlic: The most pungent member of the onion family. The heads of firm cloves should be free of any decay and green sprouts. Buy them only as needed, since their shelf life is limited. Most recipes call for one or two cloves in sauces, soups, salads, braised and sautéed dishes, and as a seasoning for roasts. The cook's discretion and individual preference will determine garlic quantities.

Green onions: Young, small onions pulled while their tops are still green; thin white bulbs are milder than the rounder, thicker ones. Use sliced in salads, sauces and oriental dishes, or try them whole, cooked in boiling salted water as you would asparagus, served with lemon-herb butter, cooked à la grecque, or beer-batter fried. Their flavor is so delicate, they can be substituted for shallots or chives whenever necessary.

Chives: Best potted or planted in an herb garden, where the slim green leaves can be snipped as needed. This diminutive herb has a delicate onion flavor that complements soups, salads, sauces, cottage cheese, eggs, herbed butter, mayonnaise and dressings.

Leeks: Resemble green onions, but larger and darker, with coarse green tops. Trim the root end and slit leek through the green tops to within ¼ inch of root. Fan the leaves open under cold running water to remove any grit. The green ends are usually used in soups and sauces; the white end plus an inch or two of the green in most other dishes. Cook trimmed leek à la grecque, braised in orange juice, or boiled and chilled and served with a vinaigrette.

Onions, Piedmont Style (Cipolle alla Piemontese)

Fragrant onions from Piedmont owe their special flavor to Italy's mineral-rich soil. Try Spanish or Bermuda onions for this dish, which can be a first course or luncheon fare.

6 servings

6 large Spanish or Bermuda onions, halved crosswise

2 tablespoons (¼ stick) unsalted butter
1 tablespoon oil
  Pinch of ground cloves

3 sweet Italian sausages

3 tablespoons freshly grated

  Parmesan cheese
  Pinch of allspice

1 egg, beaten

2¼ ounces grappa *or* vodka
2 tablespoons very fine breadcrumbs

1 cup water
2 tablespoons fresh lemon juice

Preheat oven to 375°F. Butter one or two baking dishes (large enough to accommodate onion halves in single layer). Hollow centers from onions. Coarsely chop pulp and set aside.

Melt 1 tablespoon butter with oil in large skillet over low heat. Add onion halves in batches cut side down and brown gently. Turn upright and cook 1 to 2 minutes. Transfer to prepared dish(es) and sprinkle with cloves.

Add sausages to same skillet. Prick with fork and cover with water. Cook until all water is evaporated, then let brown lightly in their own rendered fat. Drain well on paper towels and let cool.

Drain all but 1 tablespoon fat from skillet. Add chopped onion and sauté until soft and translucent. Transfer to mixing bowl. Skin sausages and crumble into bowl. Add Parmesan and pinch of allspice and blend thoroughly.

Reserve 1 tablespoon beaten egg and blend remainder into meat and onion. Divide among onion halves.

Add a little grappa or vodka to reserved egg. Brush tops of onions with mixture, then sprinkle with breadcrumbs.

Combine remaining grappa or vodka, water and lemon juice and pour around onions. Cover with foil and bake 15 minutes. Remove foil, reduce oven to 350°F and continue baking 20 minutes. Add remaining 1 tablespoon butter to liquid in dish. Baste onions and cook until all liquid is absorbed and onions are tender and moist. Serve hot or cold.

Bread and Onion Sausage (Knepfle au Torchon)

This classic Germanic dish was originally developed at a time when flour was scarce and not a single crumb of bread was to be wasted. Brioche, favored among the Christians, and challah, the traditional Jewish sabbath bread, are generally used because of their capacity to absorb the onion-flavored egg mixture. The egg-soaked crumbs are rolled in cheesecloth to form a large sausage, then poached. The cooked egg holds the crumbs together. The sausage is then sliced and sautéed in browned butter to hearty, down-to-earth perfection.

6 servings

¼ cup (½ stick) unsalted butter
2 medium onions, finely chopped
2 medium leeks (white part only), finely chopped
2 shallots, finely chopped
2 medium garlic cloves, finely chopped
Salt and freshly ground pepper

1¼ cups half and half
4 eggs
2 cups ½-inch cubes stale challah with crust, toasted until golden (about ½ loaf)

1½ tablespoons chopped fresh chives
¼ teaspoon freshly grated nutmeg

Corn oil
2 beef bouillon cubes

¼ cup (½ stick) butter, heated to dark golden and cooled

Sour cream (garnish)

Melt unsalted butter in heavy large skillet over low heat. Stir in onions, leeks, shallots and garlic. Cover and cook until vegetables are translucent, about 10 minutes. Season with salt and pepper. Remove skillet from heat.

Beat half and half with eggs in medium bowl until well blended. Stir bread cubes, chives and nutmeg into vegetables. Blend in egg mixture. Set mixture aside for about 30 minutes to allow bread cubes to absorb liquid.

Bring large amount of water to rapid boil in stockpot. Meanwhile, cut three 12 × 36-inch rectangles of cheesecloth. Stack cheesecloth to form 3 layers. Brush top layer generously with corn oil. Turn bread mixture onto cheesecloth about 6 inches from 1 short end and several inches from sides. Fold 6-inch border over, then continue to roll mixture up in cheesecloth. Twist ends to enclose bread mixture; tie securely with string. Add bouillon cubes to boiling water and stir to dissolve. Add sausage and return water to boil. Reduce heat and simmer sausage until firm to touch, about 40 minutes.

Remove sausage from water and cool to lukewarm. Remove cheesecloth. Brush sausage with some of browned butter. Set aside and let cool completely.

Cut sausage into ⅔-inch-thick slices. Reheat browned butter in heavy large skillet over medium heat. Add sausage slices (in batches if necessary) and cook until light golden. Serve immediately. Pass sour cream separately.

 # *Mushrooms*

French-Fried Mushrooms

8 servings

32 medium mushrooms
All purpose flour seasoned with salt and pepper
2 eggs beaten with 1 teaspoon water and 1 teaspoon oil

1½ cups fresh fine breadcrumbs

Oil for deep frying
Tartar Sauce (see following recipe)

Rinse mushrooms but do not dry. Dredge in seasoned flour. Dip in egg mixture until well coated. Roll in breadcrumbs. Can be refrigerated until ready for frying.

Heat oil in large skillet or deep fryer to 375°F. Fry mushrooms in batches until golden brown, 2 to 3 minutes. Drain on paper towels. Serve hot accompanied by Tartar Sauce.

Tartar Sauce

1½ cups mayonnaise
8 anchovy fillets, minced
1 hard-cooked egg, finely chopped
2 tablespoons minced fresh parsley
2 tablespoons minced capers
2 teaspoons fresh lemon juice

1 teaspoon minced onion
1 teaspoon finely snipped chives
1 teaspoon Dijon mustard
½ teaspoon dried tarragon, crumbled

Combine ingredients in medium bowl and mix well. Refrigerate until serving time.

Mustard Mushrooms

2 to 3 servings

¼ cup (½ stick) butter
½ small onion, chopped
1 pound mushrooms, sliced
⅓ cup dry vermouth

1 tablespoon Dijon mustard
Salt and freshly ground pepper

Melt butter in heavy skillet over low heat. Add onion. Cover and cook until translucent, about 10 minutes. Increase heat to medium high, add mushrooms and sauté until tender, about 5 minutes. Add vermouth and cook, stirring occasionally, until liquid is almost evaporated, about 2 minutes. Blend in mustard; do not boil. Season with salt and pepper to taste. Serve hot.

Four Mushroom and Green Onion Sauce

Poached chicken breasts or grilled veal chops are special when served with this sauce. Or add the optional Italian sausage to the sauce and toss with pasta.

Makes 2 cups

⅓ cup dried shiitake mushrooms (about 4 large)
⅓ cup cloud ears (dried black mushrooms)
¼ cup dried porcini mushrooms
1 cup boiling water

1 cup chicken stock (preferably homemade)
½ cup dry white wine
2 tablespoons sliced green onion (white part only)
¾ teaspoon minced garlic

1¾ cups whipping cream
½ cup sliced fresh mushrooms
1 tablespoon tamari soy sauce
⅜ teaspoon ground cumin
½ cup cooked Italian sausage (optional), crumbled (about 3 ounces)
3 tablespoons diagonally sliced green onion (green part only)
1½ teaspoons fresh lemon juice
Pinch of ground red pepper
Salt

Combine shiitake, cloud ears and porcini in medium bowl. Stir in boiling water. Set aside for 30 minutes to soften, stirring occasionally.

Meanwhile, combine chicken stock, white wine, white part of onion and garlic in heavy large skillet and bring to boil over medium-high heat. Let boil until reduced to about ¾ cup.

Drain mushrooms, reserving liquid. Rinse mushrooms under cold running water. Drain. Strain reserved liquid through several layers of dampened cheesecloth. Cut hard cores out of mushrooms and discard. Add liquid to sauce. Slice shiitake very thinly. Slice cloud ears and porcini coarsely. Add shiitake, cloud ears and porcini to sauce with cream, fresh mushrooms, soy sauce and cumin. Bring sauce to boil over medium-high heat. Continue boiling until reduced to 2 cups, stirring frequently. Stir in sausage, green part of onion, lemon juice and ground red pepper. Season with salt. Serve hot.

Recipe can be doubled, but use only ½ cup each shiitake and cloud ears and 6 tablespoons porcini mushrooms.

Mushroom Nachos

6 to 8 servings

24 large fresh mushrooms,* cleaned with damp paper towel
4 to 6 tablespoons (½ to ¾ stick) butter, melted

2 ounces pepperoni or chorizo sausage, halved lengthwise and thinly sliced (24 pieces)

1 to 2 jalapeño peppers, finely chopped
1½ cups shredded Monterey Jack or sharp cheddar cheese (6 ounces)
1 small red bell pepper, roasted, or 2 pimientos, cut into 24 pieces
¼ cup minced green onion

Line baking sheet with foil. Remove stems from mushrooms; reserve for another use. Brush entire surfaces of mushroom caps with melted butter. Arrange mushroom caps rounded side down on prepared baking sheet.

Preheat broiler. Set 1 piece of sausage in each mushroom cap. Sprinkle with jalapeños, then cheese. Top with red pepper or pimiento. Broil 6 inches from heat source until cheese is melted. Transfer to heated platter. Sprinkle with minced green onion and serve.

*Zucchini slices (cut ¼ inch thick) can be substituted for mushroom caps.

🍄 Mushrooms

Mushrooms add a festive note to any meal. With their subtle flavor, distinctive texture and beautiful appearance, they have a magical ability to transform even the most mundane ingredients into truly extraordinary fare.

Before the commercial cultivation of mushrooms, which began in France at the time of Louis XIV, they were so rare a delicacy in many locales that they were reserved for the ruling classes. Happily, we now have a lavish supply not only of the common cultivated variety but of some unusual newcomers from the Orient, *shiitake* and *enoki,* as well as a wider selection of dried kinds. With such bounty at hand it is a challenge to explore the whole range of mushroom cookery from garnishes and sauces to soups and main courses.

Not the least of the mushroom's benefits is the fact that it is unusually low in calories, rich in vitamins and low in sodium. Four large mushrooms contain just about three calories. So they not only make an elegant addition to main dishes, sandwiches and salads, they serve as a low-calorie extender.

When buying button mushrooms look for those that are firm, without blemishes and with caps tightly closed so that gills underneath the cap are invisible. In the East and Midwest cultivated mushrooms are snow-white, but in California and some of the other Western states white, cream-colored and brown varieties are available.

To store mushrooms, place—unwashed—in plastic container that is open at the top or in paper produce bag that is left open to allow them to breathe. Plastic bags should not be used for storage because mushrooms tend to give off moisture and they will become soggy. If you buy really fresh, firm mushrooms they can keep as long as one week. But those that are past their prime should be used as soon as possible because they lose their uniform color, firm texture and full flavor.

Mushrooms should be cleaned just before cooking or eating. If you're certain mushrooms are untreated with chemicals simply wipe them with a dampened paper towel or soft-bristle mushroom brush. If you have any uncertainty about this, it is preferable to rinse them and dry quickly on paper towels. It is not necessary to peel mushrooms; simply trim off a thin slice from the stem before using.

The temptation to gather wild mushrooms can be very strong but unless you are expert on the subject, it is almost impossible to be sure which fungi are edible and which are poisonous just by their appearance. It can cause serious and dangerous consequences.

One sometimes overlooked area of mushroom cookery that is not only safe but offers delightful new taste experiences is the use of dried mushrooms—especially Japanese, Chinese, Italian and Polish imports. In addition to convenience, the dried varieties have deliciously intense flavor. To reconstitute them, wash them first to remove dust and grit, then soak in lukewarm water to cover for approximately thirty minutes. Reserve the soaking water for use in the recipe. Or add dried mushrooms to hearty soups, sauces and dressings. They are one more proof that mushrooms are magical.

Warm Mushroom Spread

Makes about 2½ cups

4 slices bacon

8 ounces mushrooms, chopped (about 3 cups)
1 medium onion, finely chopped
1 garlic clove, minced
2 tablespoons all purpose flour
⅛ teaspoon freshly ground pepper
1 8-ounce package cream cheese, cubed

2 teaspoons Worcestershire sauce
1 teaspoon soy sauce
½ cup sour cream
1 teaspoon fresh lemon juice

Cocktail rye or assorted crackers

Cook bacon in large skillet over medium heat until crisp. Transfer to small bowl, crumble and set aside.

Pour off all but 2 tablespoons drippings from skillet. Add mushrooms, onion and garlic to skillet and sauté over medium-high heat until liquid evaporates. Stir in flour and pepper and mix well. Add cream cheese, Worcestershire sauce and soy sauce and continue cooking until cheese is melted. Blend in sour cream, lemon juice and bacon and cook until heated through; *do not boil.* Serve warm with cocktail rye or assorted crackers.

Fresh Mushrooms with Eggplant and Tomato

Makes 30 to 40 appetizers

1 1-pound eggplant
Sea salt or coarse salt

3 tablespoons olive oil (preferably cold-pressed)

1 medium-size yellow onion, finely chopped
1 large celery stalk, finely chopped
2 medium-size firm mushrooms, coarsely chopped
1½ teaspoons finely chopped garlic
Herb or vegetable salt

1 large or 2 medium-size tomatoes, peeled and coarsely chopped
2 tablespoons dry whole wheat breadcrumbs
1 tablespoon tomato paste
5 tablespoons finely chopped fresh parsley

Fresh lemon juice
30 to 40 medium-size firm mushrooms

Cut eggplant in half lengthwise. Make crisscross pattern in pulp and sprinkle with salt. Let stand 30 minutes.

Rinse eggplant thoroughly and drain well; pat dry with paper towels. Peel eggplant and coarsely chop pulp.

Heat 2 tablespoons oil in medium skillet over medium-low heat. Add eggplant and cook until softened, about 2 minutes. Remove from pan and let cool.

Heat remaining oil in same skillet over medium heat. Add onion, celery, mushroom, garlic and herb salt and cook 3 to 4 minutes. Return eggplant to skillet with tomatoes. Stir in breadcrumbs, tomato paste and 3 tablespoons parsley. Season with herb salt and continue cooking over medium heat about 4 minutes. *(Mixture can be prepared ahead to this point, covered and refrigerated.)*

Just before serving, dampen paper towel with mixture of water and small amount of lemon juice. Wipe mushrooms lightly. Carefully remove stems. Fill each cap with some of stuffing. Sprinkle with remaining parsley.

Mushrooms can also be served hot. Run under broiler or bake briefly to warm through before sprinkling with parsley.

7 ❦ Mixed Vegetables

Just as different meats and seafoods may be combined to create delicious and unusual recipes, so can vegetables be imaginatively mixed in endless variety. The recipes in this chapter are so delightfully diverse that you can find one to suit any mood or menu.

Chinese Salad, Rich Style (page 104) is a fun do-it-yourself dish for guests and would be a good way to begin a homemade oriental dinner. For more formal occasions, there are several possibilities here: Mushroom Vegetable Terrine (page 112), an eight-vegetable combination served with a homemade Tarragon-Tomato Sauce is an impressive appetizer. Gourmandise de Légumes (page 110), a spectacular presentation of four vegetable purees, would be an appropriate accompaniment to a special setting.

There are some interesting ideas for entrées, including Ticinese Vegetable Casserole and Vegetable Quiche (both page 111). Choose also from an array of easy-to-make sautés, salads, sauces and stir-frys to add a bit of zip to everyday dining. For instance, accompany simply broiled chicken or fish with Mixed Grilled Vegetables (page 111) for a change of pace. The Puree of Potatoes and Celery Root (page 107) would be marvelous with pork chops or beef.

Let these delectable mixtures inspire your own creations, too: Substitute other similar in-season vegetables for one or two in a recipe for an entirely different but equally tempting result. We think you will find that this collection offers an infinite number of possibilities.

Chinese Salad, Rich Style

Each person takes a paper-thin crepe, places some salad in the center and rolls his or her own serving. A marvelous way to start a Chinese dinner.

Makes 20 rolls

1½ cups Chinese cabbage, cut into 1-inch-long shreds *or* 1½ cups celery, cut into 1-inch-long shreds
1 ounce fresh bean sprouts
1 cup carrots, cut into 1-inch-long shreds
1 cup Chinese turnips (daikon), cut into 1-inch-long shreds
1 teaspoon salt
½ cup rehydrated cloud ears* (black tree fungus)
1 cup rehydrated cellophane noodles* (also known as bean threads)

1 cup shredded bean curd
½ cup shredded Egg Pancake (see following recipes)
½ cup shredded cooked pork
½ cup shredded cooked chicken

1½ tablespoons dry mustard
3 tablespoons light soy sauce
2 tablespoons sesame oil**
1 tablespoon vinegar
1 teaspoon sugar

20 Spring Rolls (commercial or homemade — see following recipes)

Place cabbage and bean sprouts in separate bowls. Pour boiling water over each and let stand 10 seconds. Drain thoroughly, rinse with cold water and squeeze dry. Set aside.

Place carrots and turnips in separate bowls and toss *each* with ½ teaspoon salt. Let stand 10 minutes. Rinse with cold water, drain and squeeze dry.

Mound carrot shreds in center of large serving platter. Surround with cabbage, bean sprouts, turnips, cloud ears, noodles, bean curd, Egg Pancake, pork and chicken.

In small bowl combine mustard with enough water to make paste. Cover and let stand in warm place 1 minute. Stir in soy sauce, sesame oil, vinegar and sugar.

Fold Spring Rolls into quarters. Place in steamer basket, strainer or colander, cover with lid or foil and steam over simmering water until warm.

To serve, pour sauce over vegetables and mix with chopsticks at table in front of guests. Pass Spring Rolls, allowing each person to mound some salad in center and then roll cigar fashion.

Salad and sauce can be prepared 1 day ahead, covered and refrigerated.

* To rehydrate cloud ears and cellophane noodles: Place in separate bowls, cover with boiling water and let stand until softened. Drain well. Cut into 1-inch lengths and measure ½ cup cloud ears and 1 cup noodles for use; cover any remainder and store in refrigerator.
**Available in oriental markets.

Egg Pancake

1 egg   1 egg yolk

Beat egg and yolk together in small bowl. Heat 10-inch nonstick skillet over medium-low heat. Pour in egg mixture, rotating pan to cover bottom evenly. When underside is cooked, loosen edges of pancake and gently turn to cook other side. Remove from pan and cut into shreds.

Spring Rolls

Makes about 2 dozen

2 cups all purpose flour
¾ cup boiling water

Flour
1 to 2 tablespoons sesame oil

Combine flour and water in medium bowl and mix well to form soft dough. Knead gently on lightly floured surface until smooth and elastic, about 10 minutes. Cover with damp towel and let stand 15 minutes.

Lightly flour surface and roll dough into circle ¼ inch thick. Using 2½-inch cookie cutter or glass, cut out as many circles of dough as possible. Collect scraps, knead together and roll out again to cut additional circles. Place circles side by side and brush half of them lightly with sesame oil. Lay unoiled circles on top, sandwich fashion.

Roll each "sandwich" into 6-inch circle, rotating dough as you roll so it keeps its shape. Turn once to roll other side. Cover pancakes with dry towel.

Place heavy 8-inch nonstick skillet over high heat about 30 seconds. Reduce heat to medium and cook pancakes one at a time, turning them as they puff up and little bubbles appear on surface. Regulate heat so pancakes become speckled with brown after cooking 1 minute on each side. As each pancake is finished, gently separate halves of "sandwich" and stack on plate. Serve immediately, or wrap in foil and refrigerate for later use.

Spring Rolls can be frozen. To reheat, steam 10 minutes, or wrap in foil and bake 10 minutes in 350°F oven.

Italian Pickled Vegetables (Giardinieria)

Makes 2 gallons

2 pounds zucchini, cut into ¼ × 2½-inch julienne (do not peel)
2 bunches carrots, peeled and cut into ¼ × 2½-inch julienne
1 large cauliflower, cut into small florets
1½ pounds broccoli (1 bunch), cut into florets
1 small bunch celery, cut into 1 × 3-inch strips
3 green bell peppers, cored, seeded and cut into ½-inch julienne
3 red bell peppers, cored, seeded and cut into ½-inch julienne
2 quarts water
2 cups coarse salt

4 quarts white vinegar

3 cups sugar
½ cup mustard seed
½ cup celery seed
3 tablespoons ground turmeric
2 tablespoons black peppercorns
1 16-ounce jar red and green cherry peppers, well drained
1 14-ounce can pitted black olives, well drained
1 10-ounce jar pimiento-stuffed green olives, well drained
1 10-ounce jar peperoncini,* well drained
8 bay leaves
8 large garlic cloves
8 tiny dried red chilies

Combine zucchini, carrots, cauliflower, broccoli, celery and bell peppers in 1 or 2 large bowls. Bring water to boil in medium saucepan. Add salt and stir until dissolved. Let cool. Pour cooled brine evenly over vegetables, covering completely. Let stand for at least 8 hours, preferably overnight.

Drain vegetables and rinse thoroughly in cold water. Drain well. Combine vinegar, sugar, mustard seed, celery seed, turmeric and peppercorns in stockpot and bring to rapid boil over high heat. Stir in vegetables. Add cherry peppers, black olives, green olives and peperoncini and simmer 2 minutes. Remove from heat. Using slotted spoon, pack some of vegetables into 1 clean, hot quart jar to ½ inch from top. Add 1 bay leaf, 1 garlic clove and 1 chili to jar. Ladle enough brine over mixture just to cover. Run plastic knife or spatula between vegetables and jar to release any air bubbles. Clean rim and threads of jar with damp cloth. Seal with new, scalded, very hot lid. Repeat with remaining vegetable mixture. Transfer jars to gently simmering (180°F to 190°F) water bath and process for 20 minutes. Let jars cool on rack. Test for seal. Store vegetables in cool dry place.

For vegetable variation, substitute or add trimmed tiny artichokes (parboiled for 2 minutes), tiny whole onions, fresh fennel strips, baby turnips and brussels sprouts. Adjust bay leaves, dried red chilies and garlic cloves if desired.

*Available at Italian markets.

Quick and Easy Curried Vegetables

4 servings

2 cups sliced vegetables (zucchini, broccoli, carrots, cauliflower)
1 cup plain yogurt
2 tablespoons chutney

½ to 1 tablespoon curry powder or to taste

Steam vegetables until crisp-tender. Blend remaining ingredients in small bowl. Transfer vegetables to serving bowl and spoon sauce over. Serve immediately.

Okra and Green Beans

This is even better made the night before to allow flavors to blend. Serve either warm or cold.

6 servings

¾ pound fresh okra
  Vinegar (optional)
¾ pound fresh green beans

9 ounces (1 cup plus 2 tablespoons) water
1 6-ounce can tomato paste

½ cup olive oil
1 onion, diced
2 large garlic cloves, chopped or crushed
  Salt and freshly ground pepper

Cut stems from okra; wash pods. If desired, soak okra in vinegar 30 minutes to remove some of its stickiness. Rinse well and drain. Wash beans and cut into lengths not exceeding 3 inches.

Combine water, tomato paste, olive oil, onion, garlic, salt and pepper in saucepan and mix well. Heat, stirring frequently, until mixture comes to boil. Add okra and beans and additional water if necessary to almost cover vegetables. Reduce heat to low, cover and simmer gently until vegetables are crisp-tender, 30 to 35 minutes.

Okra and Green Beans can also be tented with foil and baked in 350°F oven 30 to 40 minutes.

Linguine with Broccoli, Cauliflower and Mushrooms

8 servings

1 cup ricotta cheese
⅓ cup grated Romano cheese

1 teaspoon salt
1 medium cauliflower, cut into florets
1½ pounds broccoli (1 bunch), cut into florets

1 cup olive oil

6 garlic cloves, minced
1 pound mushrooms, thickly sliced
2 teaspoons salt
½ teaspoon dried red pepper flakes

1 pound linguine
Grated Romano cheese

Combine ricotta and Romano; set aside.

Bring large stockpot of water to rolling boil. Add salt, cauliflower and broccoli. Cover and return to boil. Uncover and cook until vegetables are crisp-tender, about 7 minutes. Remove vegetables with slotted spoon and reserve liquid for cooking linguine.

Heat olive oil and garlic in large skillet. When garlic is lightly browned, stir in mushrooms, salt and red pepper and sauté about 5 minutes. Stir in broccoli and cauliflower and continue cooking 10 minutes. If mixture becomes too dry, add some of the reserved cooking liquid.

Bring cooking liquid to rapid boil, adding water if needed. Add linguine, stirring with fork to prevent sticking, and cook until al dente, about 10 to 12 minutes. Drain well. Reheat vegetable mixture; stir in linguine. Divide among shallow bowls and top with cheese mixture. Dust with more Romano.

Green Beans with Cherry Tomatoes

2 servings

⅓ pound fresh green beans, ends trimmed

4 to 6 cherry tomatoes, halved

1 tablespoon butter
1 tablespoon minced fresh parsley
Salt and freshly ground pepper

Cut beans diagonally into 1-inch pieces. Transfer to saucepan and cover with boiling salted water. Boil uncovered 5 minutes. Cover and continue cooking until just tender, about 10 more minutes. Drain well.

Transfer beans to serving bowl. Add remaining ingredients and toss gently. Serve immediately.

Puree of Potatoes and Celery Root

4 servings

4 large boiling potatoes, peeled and quartered
3 medium celery roots, peeled and quartered
2 tablespoons chopped onion

Salt and freshly ground pepper
Butter

Paprika and snipped chives or chopped green onion (garnish)

Combine potatoes and celery root in steamer or saucepan and sprinkle with onion. Steam until very tender when pierced with fork, about 20 to 25 minutes.

Transfer to processor or blender. Sprinkle with salt and pepper and dot with butter. Puree until smooth. Turn into serving dish and garnish liberally with paprika and chives or green onion.

🍎 *Vegetables Seasonality Chart*

Vegetable	Season	Look For
Artichokes	October to June; peak months: April, May	Tight, plump green buds heavy for their size
Jerusalem Artichokes	October to March	Firm, unscarred tubers with tender beige-to-brown skins
Asparagus	Late February to July; peak months: April, May	Straight, bright green stalks of uniform size with tight tips and moist bases
Beans	Summer for Italian green beans, black-eyed peas. Year round for all others	Firm, well-filled pods; wax and green beans should be of uniform size and fairly straight
Beets	Year round; peak months for greens and beets: June to October	Crisp-tender greens; firm and unscarred of equal size 1½-2″ in diameter
Broccoli	Year round with best supplies in spring and fall	Crisp, moist stalks and dark green or purplish heads. Reject any that are yellowed or flowering
Brussels Sprouts	September to March; peak months: October and November	Firm, clean compact heads of a crisp green color
Cabbage	Year round for all cabbages	Firm, heavy heads with crisp, unblemished leaves. Green cabbages fade in storage, so avoid white heads
Carrots	Year round	Firm and bright orange without cracks or splits. If buying by the bunch, avoid wilted tops
Cauliflower	Year round; peak months: September to December	Snowy, compact heads with crisp green leaves and few or no dark spots. Reject any open, spongy heads
Celery	Year round	Crunchy stalks with crisp, green leaves. Avoid stalks with cracks or bruises
Chard	June to November	Crisp leaves and fleshy stalks
Corn	May to October; available year round, but best in summer	Ears in the husk preferably from iced bins; husks should be bright green and snug-fitting; kernels plump and milky
Cucumbers	Year round	Firm and green with no dark, soft spots

Vegetable	Season	Look For
Eggplant	Year round	Firm and evenly purple without cuts or scars, that weigh heavy for their size
Leeks	Year round; two peak seasons: September to December and April to July	Fresh green tops and crisp, white clean stalks
Mushrooms	Year round though supplies may be short in summer	Clean, snowy and plump of uniform size; the veil that joins cap to stem should be intact
Onions	Year round for red, white, and yellow onions; March to June for Bermudas; and August to May for Spanish onions	Firm and well-shaped with dry, clean, bright skins; reject any that are sprouting
Peas	Year round for all peas; peak season April to August	Bright green, tender pods; green pea pods should be well filled, snow pea pods slender and crisp
Peppers	Year round for all; peak season: June to October	Bright, firm fleshy pods
Pumpkin	Autumn	Small, firm and bright orange, about 6-7″ in diameter, that weigh heavy for their size
Spinach	Year round; peak months: March to July	Crisp, dark green and moist leaves with roots attached. If buying prewashed, bagged spinach, be sure it's not wilted, slimy or dry
Summer Squash (Yellow Squash, Pattypan and Zucchini)	Year round for all three types	Firm, tender skinned and blemish-free that weigh heavy for their size
Winter Squash (Acorn Squash, Butternut, Buttercup, Hubbard)	Year round for acorn squash; fall and winter for the others	Heavy with hard, clean unblemished skins
Tomatoes	Year round but best in summer	Firm and well-formed of good strong color (whether red, green or yellow) with smooth, unblemished skins
Turnips	Year round; peak season: fall	Firm and smooth; 2-3″ across with few leaf scars or roots

Rainbow of Four Vegetable Purees
(Gourmandise de Légumes)

6 servings

2 medium turnips, peeled and chopped
2 large or 3 medium carrots, chopped
1 bunch broccoli (1½ pounds), florets only
Salt and freshly ground white pepper

1 pound mushrooms, finely chopped
1 tablespoon butter

Custard
1 cup whipping cream
1 egg
2 egg yolks
1 tablespoon fresh lemon juice
Dash of freshly grated nutmeg

Hollandaise Sauce (see following recipe) (optional)

Cook turnips, carrots and broccoli separately in boiling salted water until very tender. Drain and dry on paper towels. Puree each in processor or blender until smooth. Return to pans and cook over low heat to remove any excess moisture. Measure 1 cup of each puree and season with salt and pepper to taste.

Squeeze mushrooms in corner of a towel to remove excess moisture. Melt butter in skillet over medium heat. Add mushrooms and cook until almost black and moisture has evaporated. Measure 1 cup and season with salt and freshly ground pepper to taste.

For custard: Combine ingredients in medium bowl and beat just until smooth. Add about 2 tablespoons to turnip puree, or just enough to make thick, smooth paste. Repeat with carrot, broccoli and mushrooms.

Preheat oven to 350°F. Generously butter six ½-cup timbale molds or soufflé dishes. Using pastry bag fitted with ¼-inch plain tip (or 20-inch piece of parchment or heavy-duty foil shaped into cone), pipe turnip puree into each mold until ¼ full. Smooth surface with back of spoon and tap molds on counter to distribute puree evenly. Repeat procedure with carrot, then broccoli, and finish with mushrooms, smoothing and tapping molds after each is added.

Set in deep baking pan and add boiling water to come within ½ inch from top of molds. Cover with parchment or foil and bake 30 minutes. Remove from water bath and let stand 10 minutes. Invert onto plates and serve with Hollandaise Sauce if desired.

Hollandaise Sauce

4 egg yolks
1 tablespoon lemon juice
¼ teaspoon salt
Dash of freshly ground white pepper

½ cup (1 stick) butter, heated until sizzling
½ cup Chablis or other dry white wine, heated

Combine yolks, lemon juice, salt and pepper in blender and mix well. With motor on high, begin adding butter drop by drop, then in thin steady stream, and blend until sauce is thickened. Pour in wine and serve at once.

Mixed Grilled Vegetables (Escalibada)

8 servings

Olive oil
8 thin young Japanese eggplants
4 large red or green bell peppers
4 large jalapeño peppers (optional)
4 large tomatoes, halved

4 medium-size white onions, halved
4 large baking potatoes, halved

Salt and freshly ground pepper

Chopped fresh parsley (garnish)

Preheat oven to 350°F or prepare barbecue. Rub olive oil over eggplants, bell peppers, jalapeño peppers, tomatoes, onions and potatoes. Transfer vegetables to baking sheet or grill. Cook until just tender, about 15 minutes for tomatoes, 30 minutes for peppers, 30 minutes to 1 hour for eggplants (depending on size), 1 hour for potatoes and 1¼ hours for onions. Remove from oven and let cool.

Peel and slice eggplants and peppers into ¼-inch strips. Season vegetables with olive oil, salt and pepper to taste. Arrange vegetables decoratively on large platter. Garnish with parsley. Serve warm or at room temperature.

Ticinese Vegetable Casserole (Smeazza)

6 to 8 servings

6 large leeks, trimmed and chopped
1 pound chopped fresh spinach
1 cup finely chopped Swiss chard
3 eggs, beaten
1 tablespoon all purpose flour
1 tablespoon cornmeal
1 teaspoon salt
½ teaspoon freshly ground pepper

¼ pound grated cheese (Gruyère, Sbrinz, Fontina, Tilsit or any combination)
¼ cup plus 1 tablespoon butter, cut into pieces

Butter 2-quart baking dish. Preheat oven to 350°F. Combine leek, spinach and chard in large bowl. Combine beaten eggs, flour, cornmeal, salt and pepper in another large bowl and mix well. Add egg mixture to vegetables. Stir in grated cheese. Pour into prepared dish. Dot with butter. Bake until center is firm, about 20 to 30 minutes.

Vegetable Quiche

6 to 8 servings

Pastry
⅓ cup shortening
1 cup self-rising flour
2 to 3 tablespoons cold water

Filling
⅓ cup diced carrot
⅓ cup diced celery
⅓ cup chopped onion
⅓ cup diced broccoli
⅓ cup diced cauliflower
⅓ cup diced zucchini
Oil

4 eggs, lightly beaten
2 cups whipping cream or half and half
1½ cups shredded Swiss cheese
¼ teaspoon salt
¼ teaspoon freshly ground white pepper
¼ teaspoon garlic powder
¼ teaspoon freshly grated nutmeg
¼ cup blanched sliced almonds

For pastry: Preheat oven to 325°F. Cut shortening into flour until mixture resembles coarse meal. Sprinkle in water one tablespoon at a time, mixing until dough pulls cleanly away from sides of bowl.

Form dough into ball, then flatten on lightly floured board. Roll dough into circle 2 inches larger than inverted 9-inch pie pan. Ease crust into pan; trim and flute edge.

For filling: Sauté vegetables in small amount of oil until crisp-tender. Transfer to bowl using slotted spoon and let cool.

Combine remaining ingredients except almonds. Pour over vegetables and stir to coat evenly. Pour into crust and sprinkle with almonds. Bake 1 hour, or until knife inserted in center comes out clean. Let cool 10 minutes and serve.

Mushroom Vegetable Terrine

18 appetizer servings

¼ pound dried garbanzo beans (chick-peas), soaked in cold water overnight

2 tablespoons light vegetable oil (preferably cold-pressed safflower)
¼ cup unflavored gelatin
¼ cup whole wheat pastry flour
1 cup milk or reconstituted nonfat dry milk

18 fresh green beans, trimmed
9 3 × ½-inch carrot sticks
9 3 × ½-inch turnip sticks
9 6-inch fresh spinach leaves (or more)
6 to 8 fresh artichoke bottoms, cooked, or one 17½-ounce can, drained

1½ pounds mushrooms, finely chopped

3 eggs, beaten
½ cup fresh whole wheat breadcrumbs or small cubes
¼ cup finely chopped shallot
2 tablespoons light vegetable oil (preferably cold-pressed safflower) *or* unsalted butter
1 tablespoon chopped fresh tarragon or 1 teaspoon dried, crumbled
1 teaspoon finely chopped garlic
1 teaspoon mace
½ teaspoon freshly grated nutmeg
Herb or vegetable salt
Freshly ground white pepper

1 bunch watercress (garnish)

Tarragon-Tomato Sauce (see following recipe)

Combine garbanzos and soaking liquid in large saucepan. Cover and cook over medium-high heat until tender, about 3½ hours. Drain; reserve ¾ cup cooking liquid. Transfer garbanzos to processor. Add ¼ cup cooking liquid and puree until smooth.

Bring remaining ½ cup garbanzo cooking liquid and 2 tablespoons vegetable oil to boil over medium heat in small saucepan. Remove from heat. Combine gelatin and flour in small bowl. Add to cooking liquid and stir until smooth. Blend in milk. Return to heat and stir until mixture comes to boil and thickens. Freeze until just set, about 7 to 10 minutes.

Blanch beans in steamer or boiling water. Repeat with carrot and turnip sticks. Drain vegetables well and pat dry with paper towels. Dip spinach leaves in boiling water until wilted and remove immediately. Spread leaves on paper towels and pat dry. Wrap carrot and turnip sticks in spinach leaves and trim ends. Cut each artichoke bottom horizontally into 3 slices. Set aside.

Squeeze mushrooms dry in paper towels or cloth, twisting to remove as much liquid as possible. Combine mushrooms, garbanzo puree, eggs, breadcrumbs, gelatin mixture, shallot, 2 tablespoons vegetable oil or butter, tarragon, garlic, mace and nutmeg in large bowl of electric mixer and beat well. Season with herb salt and white pepper.

Preheat oven to 350°F. Coat 6- or 8-cup pâté mold or loaf pan with vegetable oil. Spread about ⅕ mushroom mixture in thin layer over bottom of pan. Arrange green beans lengthwise over top in rows. Spread another thin layer of mushroom mixture (about ⅕) over beans. Arrange half of artichoke slices over top. Add another thin layer of mushroom mixture. Arrange alternating rows of spinach-wrapped carrot and turnip sticks over top. Spread with thin layer of mushroom mixture. Add remaining artichoke slices. Spread remaining mushroom mixture over top of artichokes.

Top mold with firm-fitting lid or cover top of mold tightly with waxed paper and then aluminum foil, crimping edges to make tight seal. Set mold in roasting pan. Pour in enough hot water to come halfway up sides of mold. Bake until set, about 1½ hours. Discard wrapping. Let cool slightly. Cover with waxed paper and weight with heavy object (a brick wrapped in aluminum foil works well). Refrigerate overnight.

Run sharp knife around edge of mold (if necessary, dip pan in hot water 1 minute to loosen). Invert onto chilled serving platter. Garnish with watercress. Ladle Tarragon-Tomato Sauce over top or pass separately.

Can be refrigerated for up to 1 week.

Tarragon-Tomato Sauce

Makes 1½ cups

2 large tomatoes, peeled, halved and seeded
¼ cup chopped yellow onion
2 tablespoons tomato paste
2 tablespoons finely chopped fresh tarragon or 1 tablespoon dried, crumbled

Herb or vegetable salt
Freshly ground white pepper

Combine tomatoes and onion in processor or blender and puree until smooth. Add tomato paste and tarragon and mix well. Season with herb salt and white pepper to taste.

Sauce can be refrigerated up to 1 week.

Vegetable Julienne Stir-Fry

4 servings

¼ cup peanut oil
1 bunch broccoli stems, peeled and sliced into 2-inch julienne
2 medium carrots, peeled and sliced into 2-inch julienne

½ small celery root (9 ounces), peeled and sliced into 2-inch julienne
4 teaspoons fresh lemon juice
Salt and freshly ground pepper

Heat oil in heavy large skillet or deep fryer to 300°F. Add vegetables and stir-fry until crisp-tender, about 3 minutes. Transfer to platter using slotted spoon. Sprinkle with lemon juice and salt and pepper. Serve hot or cold.

Broccoli and Cauliflower with Lemon and Garlic

8 to 10 servings

1 large cauliflower
1 large bunch broccoli

4 to 6 tablespoons light-bodied olive oil
4 garlic cloves, chopped

½ cup water or chicken stock

Salt and freshly ground pepper

Juice of 1 lemon

½ teaspoon finely grated lemon peel (optional)

Separate cauliflower into florets. Trim tough stems from broccoli and discard. Slice remaining stems into thin rounds. Break florets into small pieces. Rinse vegetables under cold running water and drain thoroughly.

Heat oil in wok or large skillet over medium-high heat. Add garlic and cook until golden; *do not overcook or dish will be bitter.* Remove immediately with slotted spoon and set aside.

Increase heat to high. Add cauliflower and broccoli and stir-fry 2 minutes, being careful not to break florets.

Add water or stock and mix well. Cover and cook until vegetables are crisp-tender, about 2 to 3 minutes, adding more liquid if needed to prevent burning. *(Do not overcook; vegetables should be crisp-tender.)* Remove lid and continue cooking several seconds to evaporate remaining liquid. Add salt and pepper. *(Can be prepared 1 day ahead up to this point and stored in refrigerator. About 5 minutes before serving, turn vegetables into wok or skillet and stir-fry quickly over high heat with reserved garlic and lemon juice.)*

Mix in garlic and lemon juice. Place in preheated serving dish. Sprinkle with lemon peel if desired.

Bangkok Stir-Fried Vegetables (Pak Pad)

4 servings

2 to 3 tablespoons fish sauce (nam pla)*
1 tablespoon fresh lime juice
1 teaspoon sugar
½ teaspoon cornstarch
¼ teaspoon freshly ground pepper
2 tablespoons vegetable oil
1 medium onion, slivered
3 medium garlic cloves, very thinly sliced

1 cup 1-inch-long broccoli florets, blanched until crisp-tender and drained
1 cup cauliflower florets, blanched until crisp-tender and drained
1 15-ounce can tiny corn kernels, drained
½ cup bean sprouts (about 1 ounce)
1 jalapeño chili, seeded and slivered

Blend fish sauce, lime juice, sugar, cornstarch and freshly ground pepper in small bowl. Heat oil in wok over medium-high heat. Add onion and stir-fry until lightly golden. Add garlic and stir-fry until garlic is just cooked. Increase heat to high, add broccoli and cauliflower and stir-fry 3 minutes. Add corn and bean sprouts and stir-fry 2 more minutes. Pour fish sauce mixture over vegetables and blend well. Add chili, reduce heat to medium and cook, stirring constantly, until sauce thickens and coats vegetables. Serve hot.

* Available in Asian markets.

❦ Index

Credits and Acknowledgments

The following people contributed the recipes included in this book:

Auberge Mourrachonne, Mouans-Sartoux, France, Guy Tircon and Jean André, chef-owners
Melissa Smith Baker
Barrows House, Dorset, Vermont, Sally Hicks, chef; Charles and Marilyn Schubert, innkeepers
James Beard
Nancy Behrman
Terry Bell
The Berghoff, Chicago, Illinois
Susan Biggs
Johanne Blais
Jennifer Brennan
Sandra Brown
Sharon Cadwallader
Anna Teresa Callen
Judith Carrington
Elyn and Phil Clarkson
Barbara Cohen
Karen Cole
Dinah Corley
Maggi Dahlgren
Anne Darby
Déjà-Vu, Philadelphia, Pennsylvania, Salomon Montezinos, chef-owner
Debbie Durham
Robert Ehrman and Ray Henderson
The Elegant Attic, Tahoe City, California
Ernie's, San Francisco, California, Jacky Robert, chef; Victor and Roland Gotti, owners
Rodney Eubanks
Joe Famularo
Carol Field
Cindy Freeman
Garret Hill Lodge, North River, New York
Gaylord Restaurant, New York, New York
Shelley Gillette
Peggy Glass
Marion Gorman
Bob and Beverly Green
Freddy Greenberg
Connie Grisby
Laura Gulotta
Carolyn Hall
Phyllis Hanes
Zack Hanle
Rita Holmberg
Ellie Johnson
Jane Helsel Joseph
Madeleine Kamman
Lynne Kasper

Sophie Kay
Margaret H. Koehler
Loni Kuhn
Dona Kuryanowicz
La Côte Basque, New York, New York, Jean-Jacques Rachou, chef-owner
Rita Leinwand
Leith's Restaurant, London, England
Dani Manilla
Ivy Elinoff Marwil
Carmela Meely
Perla Meyers
Jinx and Jefferson Morgan
Jane Ellen Murray
Mae Norris
Jacques Pépin
Lisa Rabon
Anne Ross
Salem Cross Inn, West Brookfield, Massachusetts
Richard Sax
Norma Schechner
Selena's, Tampa, Florida
Jan Shannon
Joan Shaw
Sharron Sheehy
Edena Sheldon
Shirley Slater
Leon Soniat
Spago, Los Angeles, California, Wolfgang Puck, chef-owner
Dorothy Stewart
Marimar Torres
Turnagain, Friday Harbor, Washington, Larry Backlund, chef
Sonia Uvezian
Village House and Garden, Los Gatos, California
Jan Weimer
Audrey White
Anne Willan
Al and Katherine Williams
Gahan Wilson and Nancy Winters
Yamato, Los Angeles, California

Additional text was supplied by:

Laura Gulotta, *Eggplant*
Lynne Kasper, *Asparagus*
Rita Leinwand, *Artichokes, Cabbage*
Abby Mandel, *Onions, Mushrooms*
Jinx Morgan, *Beans, Stuffed Vegetables, Know Your Chilies*
Nancy Roberts, *Seasonality Chart*

Accessories information
for cover and two-page color spread by Dan Wolfe

Lancaster pattern English Ironstone covered vegetable tureen, dinner plate, rectangular octagonal platter and serving dish by Adams for Wedgwood, courtesy Geary's, 351 North Beverly Drive, Beverly Hills, California, 90210.

Handpainted ceramic bowl, oval platter and square serving dish are crafted by Cosenostre Grazia ceramicists and imported from Italy, courtesy La Porcelaine Blanche, 342 North Beverly Drive, Beverly Hills, California, 90210.

Oval reed basket-tray, white porcelain salt and pepper shakers, porcelain cruets courtesy Williams-Sonoma, P.O. Box 7456, San Francisco, California, 94120.

White glazed tiles courtesy International Tile Corporation, 1288 South La Brea Avenue, Los Angeles, California, 90019.

Special thanks to:

Marilou Vaughan,
    Editor, Bon Appétit
Bernard Rotondo,
    Art Director, Bon Appétit
William J. Garry,
    Managing Editor, Bon Appétit
Barbara Varnum,
    Articles Editor, Bon Appétit
Laurie Glenn Buckle,
    Associate Editor, Bon Appétit
Brenda Koplin,
    Copy Editor, Bon Appétit
Leslie A. Dame,
    Assistant Editor, Bon Appétit
Robin G. Richardson,
    Research Coordinator, Bon Appétit
Patrick R. Casey,
    Vice-President, Production, Knapp Communications Corporation
Anthony P. Iacono,
    Vice-President, Manufacturing, Knapp Communications Corporation
Philip Kaplan,
    Vice-President, Graphics, Knapp Communications Corporation
Donna Clipperton,
    Manager, Rights and Permissions, Knapp Communications Corporation
Karen Legier,
    Rights and Permissions Coordinator, Knapp Communications Corporation
Linda Greer French
Rose Grant
Edena Sheldon
Sylvia Tidwell

The Knapp Press
is a wholly owned subsidiary of
KNAPP COMMUNICATIONS CORPORATION.
Chairman and Chief Executive Officer:
Cleon T. Knapp
President: H. Stephen Cranston
Senior Vice-Presidents:
Paige Rense *(Editor-in-Chief)*
Everett T. Alcan *(Corporate Planning)*
Rosalie Bruno *(New Venture Development)*
Harry Myers *(Magazine Group Publisher)*
Betsy Wood Knapp *(MIS Electronic Media)*
L. James Wade, Jr. *(Finance)*

THE KNAPP PRESS

President: Alice Bandy; *Administrative Assistant:* Beth Bell; *Senior Editor:* Norman Kolpas; *Associate Editors:* Jeff Book, Jan Koot, Sarah Lifton, Pamela Mosher; *Editor, Gault Millau:* Deborah Patton; *Assistant Editors:* Taryn Bigelow, Colleen Dunn, Jan Stuebing; *Editorial Assistant:* Nancy D. Roberts; *Art Director:* Paula Schlosser; *Designers:* Robin Murawski, Nan Oshin; *Book Production Manager:* Larry Cooke; *Production Coordinator:* Joan Valentine; *Managing Director, Rosebud Books:*

Robert Groag; *Financial Manager:* Joseph Goodman; *Financial Analyst:* Carlton Joseph; *Assistant Finance Manager:* Kerri Culbertson; *Fulfillment Services Manager:* Virginia Parry; *Director of Public Relations:* Jan B. Fox; *Promotions Manager:* Jeanie Gould; *Promotions Coordinator:* Joanne Denison; *Marketing Assistant:* Dolores Briqueleur; *Special Sales:* Lynn Blocker; *Department Secretaries:* Amy Hershman, Randy Levin

This book is set in Sabon, a face designed by Jan Teischold in 1967 and based on early fonts engraved by Garamond and Granjon.

Composition was on the Mergenthaler Linotron 202 by Graphic Typesetting Service.

Series design by Paula Schlosser. Page layout by Betty Shimotsuka. Text stock: Glatfelter Offset Basis 65. Color plate stock: Mead Northcote Basis 70. Both furnished by WWF Paper Corporation West.

Color separations by NEC Incorporated.

Printing and binding by R.R. Donnelley and Sons.